DotNetNuke Skinning Tutorial

A simple, clear, step-by-step tutorial to creating DotNetNuke skins to put you in control of the look and feel of your DotNetNuke website

Darren Neese

PUBLISHING

BIRMINGHAM - MUMBAI

DotNetNuke Skinning Tutorial

First published: May 2008

Production Reference: 1140508

Published by Packt Publishing Ltd.
32 Lincoln Road
Olton
Birmingham, B27 6PA, UK.

ISBN 978-1-847192-78-3

www.packtpub.com

Cover Image by Vinayak Chittar (vinayak.chittar@gmail.com)

Credits

Author

Darren Neese

Reviewers

Cuong Quoc Dang

Jerry Spohn

Senior Acquisition Editor

Douglas Paterson

Development Editor

Ved Prakash Jha

Technical Editor

Mithun Sehgal

Editorial Team Leader

Mithil Kulkarni

Project Manager

Abhijeet Deobhakta

Project Coordinator

Lata Basantani

Indexer

Hemangini Bari

Proofreader

Camille Guy

Production Coordinator

Shantanu Zagade

Cover Work

Shantanu Zagade

About the Author

Darren Neese is a Microsoft specialist who currently works as a senior web developer and project manager. With over ten years of experience in the IT industry, he has worked as a Windows developer, a web developer, a database administrator, a corporate trainer, an academic teacher, as well as being a server and network administrator. He holds several related Microsoft certifications and implements DotNetNuke and other Microsoft-based solutions for clients.

I would like to thank all my friends and family who have been a great source of encouragement. I'd also like to thank Douglas Paterson who gave me lots of advice and direction during the formative stages of this book.

About the Reviewers

Cuong Quoc Dang is the Marketing Creative Director at Engage Software. His responsibilities at Engage include marketing, branding, design, and of course DotNetNuke skinning.

His priority at Engage is to provide not just a high quality DotNetNuke skin, but a full package that includes strict attention to detail in user interface design and user experience. Cuong has worked with web standards for over four years.

As an essential part of the team at Engage, Cuong has been exposed to every part of the very developer-oriented DotNetNuke community. As the lead instructor for the DotNetNuke Skinning training at Engage, Cuong is working to fulfill his mission to open up the DotNetNuke community to not only for developers, but also for designers.

In addition to helping build solid, scalable websites and applications for both Engage Software and its clients, he manages the company's two public websites, `www.engagesoftware.com` and `www.engagemodules.com`. His role also oversees the online marketing and branding initiatives.

Prior to joining Engage, Cuong worked for a logistic company in Vietnam, MinhPhuong Co., Ltd., as an Executive Marketing & Business Development. Cuong earned his Bachelor of Science in Marketing and Management from Maryville University.

Cuong Dang is currently working and living in St. Louis, MO with his wife, Vanda.

Jerry Spohn has been working with computers since the age of 11, at which he first began learning programming on a Commodore VIC 20. Times have changed, and he moved through the interesting world of IBM mainframes into PCs. After taking numerous courses on database design, programming, and object-oriented methodologies, he moved into Visual Basic and other Microsoft languages.

Jerry currently works as a Development Manager for a medium-sized software company in Pennsylvania. He also manages over 25 different websites using DotNetNuke, and is the owner of Spohn Software LLC, which does custom development across the entire Microsoft development toolset.

Table of Contents

Preface

DotNetNuke is an open-source web application framework written in VB.NET for the ASP.NET framework. The application's content management system is extensible and customizable through the use of skins and modules, and it can be used to create, deploy, and manage intranet, extranet, and websites.

DotNetNuke has a skinning architecture which provides a clear separation between design and content, enabling a web designer to develop skins without requiring any specialist knowledge of development in ASP.NET—only knowledge of HTML and an understanding of how to prepare and package the skins themselves is required.

If you want to create great looking skins for your DotNetNuke websites, this book is for you. If you're new to DotNetNuke skinning, this book is the ideal introduction. This book will give you clear, concise, and practical guidance to take you from the basics of DotNetNuke skinning right through to developing the skills to make you a DotNetNuke skinner to be reckoned with!

This book gives you step-by-step instructions to the fundamentals of skinning so that you will be in control of the look and feel of your DotNetNuke site, and dreaming of new ideas for creating more interactive user interfaces.

What This Book Covers

Chapter 1 introduces readers to the basics of DNN skinning.

Chapter 2 takes you through setting up the skin development environment and creating your first skin.

Chapter 3 deals with giving the skin we created in *Chapter 2* some structure and layout.

Chapter 4 adds style to our skin and provides information on how CSS works and cascades in DotNetNuke.

Chapter 5 explains about the skin objects and how to customize them in the proper way.

Chapter 6 details how to configure the menu in our skin. Readers will understand what attributes can be configured with the menu and its related provider.

Chapter 7 enhances your skin design by preparing and adding images to our skin.

Chapter 8 walks you through the creation of containers.

Chapter 9 shows you how to package and deploy the skins.

Chapter 10 deals with the skinning of a core component of DotNetNuke—the control panel.

What You Need for This Book
The following is what you require to work through this book:

- Version 2.0 of the .NET framework installed.
- A working DNN site with DNN starter kits installed
- Visual Web Developer and SQL Server installed

Who is This Book For
This book is for web developers who are interested in customizing the look and feel of a DotNetNuke website.

This book is ideal for beginners to DotNetNuke skinning.

You will need to know about the general operation of DotNetNuke, but also have some familiarity with creating web pages. Familiarity with CSS and basic ASP.NET would be a bonus.

Conventions
In this book, you will find a number of styles of text that distinguish between different kinds of information. Here are some examples of these styles, and an explanation of their meaning.

There are three styles for code. Code words in text are shown as follows: "After you add the id and runat attributes, take out the [CONTROLPANEL] text."

A block of code will be set as follows:

```
<tr>
  <td align="center" valign="top"
      id="TopPane" runat="server"></td>
</tr>
```

When we wish to draw your attention to a particular part of a code block, the relevant lines or items will be made bold:

```
<tr>
  <td></td>
  <td align="center" valign="top"
      id="TopPane" runat="server"></td>
  <td></td>
</tr>
```

New terms and **important words** are introduced in a bold-type font. Words that you see on the screen, in menus or dialog boxes for example, appear in our text like this: "Click on **Downloads** and download the latest version of the starter kit."

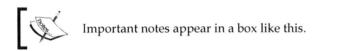 Important notes appear in a box like this.

Reader Feedback

Feedback from our readers is always welcome. Let us know what you think about this book, what you liked or may have disliked. Reader feedback is important for us to develop titles that you really get the most out of.

To send us general feedback, simply drop an email to feedback@packtpub.com, making sure to mention the book title in the subject of your message.

If there is a book that you need and would like to see us publish, please send us a note in the **SUGGEST A TITLE** form on www.packtpub.com or email to suggest@packtpub.com.

If there is a topic that you have expertise in and you are interested in either writing or contributing to a book, see our author guide on www.packtpub.com/authors.

Customer Support

Now that you are the proud owner of a Packt book, we have a number of things to help you to get the most from your purchase.

Downloading the Example Code for the Book

Visit http://www.packtpub.com/files/code/2783_Code.zip to directly download the example code.

The downloadable files contain instructions on how to use them.

Errata

Although we have taken every care to ensure the accuracy of our contents, mistakes do happen. If you find a mistake in one of our books—maybe a mistake in text or code—we would be grateful if you would report this to us. By doing this you can save other readers from frustration, and help to improve subsequent versions of this book. If you find any errata, report them by visiting http://www.packtpub.com/support, selecting your book, clicking on the **let us know** link, and entering the details of your errata. Once your errata are verified, your submission will be accepted and the errata added to the list of existing errata. The existing errata can be viewed by selecting your title from http://www.packtpub.com/support.

Questions

You can contact us at questions@packtpub.com if you are having a problem with some aspect of the book, and we will do our best to address it.

1
Overview of DNN Skinning

If you've developed a website for your employer, a client, or even your friends, you will soon notice how critical the layout, graphics, fonts, and colors are to everyone involved. Your site is quickly sized up by the first impression—'wow' factor—despite what content or functionality is or is not there. Face it, everyone gets awfully *skin*-deep superficial when it comes to websites. When it comes to DotNetNuke, a skin is the look and feel of your portal. A skin can be the determining factor on whether your DotNetNuke portal is accepted or not.

This chapter is an overview of skinning. We'll start off by describing what skinning is, what skins are made of, and what we have to work with, right after you install DotNetNuke. After reading this chapter, you will know the steps involved in skinning and also what can be done with skinning.

What is Skinning

First of all, a skin is a set of graphics, fonts, colors, and page layout defined all-in-one package to be applied to a DotNetNuke site or even just to a single page. Skinning does not have anything to do with adding content or function to a DotNetNuke site.

Skinning is the act of creating such a package. It involves creating or altering web files that are eventually zipped into a file and uploaded to a DotNetNuke site, which can then be put into action. By the end of this book, you will be well-versed in all the aspects of this rewarding process.

What are Skins Made Of

Skins are made of HTML (hyper-text markup language), CSS (cascading style sheets), *skin objects* and *panes*. Notice the following screenshot. It is a look at the typical home page once you log in to the site with the administrative privileges.

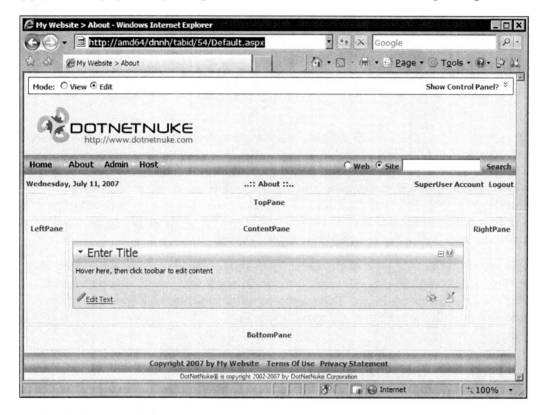

The HTML and the CSS in a skin play the same role that they would in any other non-DotNetNuke site. In this default blue skin, there are nested HTML tables structuring the page into interwoven columns and rows. The CSS defines the colors, images, and fonts used.

The skin objects are bits of functionality that almost any site needs. Notice the skin objects from top to bottom:

- logo
- menu
- search box
- current date

- breadcrumb (where it says **About**, indicating what page you are on and where are you in the menu structure)
- username link
- login/logout link
- copyright notice
- **Terms Of Use** link
- **Privacy Statement** link
- DotNetNuke copyright

Panes are the sections of a skin which serve as containers for modules you add to a page. There is one module on this particular page, titled **Enter Title**. It is in a pane appropriately named **ContentPane**. There are four other panes not being used, as you can see: **TopPane**, **LeftPane**, **RightPane**, and **BottomPane**.

As we move through the chapters together, we'll become intimately aware about how these components of the skin work together and how to customize them exactly as we want them to appear.

The Default Skins

When you install DotNetNuke, you will essentially be looking at one skin. There may technically be more than one skin, but it's just the same skin in various colors and/or forms.

As a skinner in training, you are attentive to these default skins because they are decent skin examples, and more importantly, a great place to start from to create your next skin. Eventually, you will create your own template or set of files (starting point), but we will spend some time looking at these basic skins and learn from them.

Where are Skins Located

Generally, all skins are located in the following path in your DotNetNuke install: `~\Portals\_default\Skins\`. The tilde is commonly used to refer 'where it is that you installed,' or in this case, the root of your DNN install. If you go there now and look at the **DNN-Blue** skin, you will see the following in the Windows Explorer:

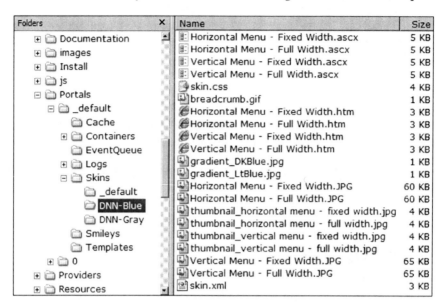

File Types in Skins

You see these typical file types in any skin:

- HTM—This is the one file type that we'll be working with, adding to, and modifying the most. While uploading a skin, this file is parsed to make the ASCX file.

- ASCX—This is the main skin file that DotNetNuke uses to apply to a site or page. There are exceptions, but this is a file you will not create yourself. DotNetNuke takes your HTM file and *parses* it into the ASCX. This file is replaced if the HTM file is re-parsed. Unless you know why you're doing it, do not create or modify this file.

- CSS—Cascading Style Sheet file. Your styles (look and feel for the common web user-interface elements) should be defined here, just like in any web application.

- XML—This holds all the attribute/value pairs to insert into the asp.net server elements/controls as DotNetNuke parses your HTM file to make the ASCX file.
- JPG/GIF/PNG—Graphics files. These are image/graphic files you will include, along with the other files, to constitute your design. (The files prefixed with 'thumbnail_' serve as small previews as to what the portal will look like if you apply it. You can see this if you go to the skins menu item on either the **Admin** or **Host** pull-down menu.)

An Overview of the Skinning Process

Here are the steps involved in creating a skin:

1. Create a folder on the file system for the skin
2. Create the files which will define the skin (htm, css, xml, etcetera)
3. Prepare the images that will be used
4. Define the layout structure with HTML and CSS
5. Link in the images
6. Designate what panes you want and where they will be
7. Insert the skin objects
8. Customize and tweak until it looks right
9. Package the skin for deployment

These steps are done in what we will call a development environment. We will not do this on the target DotNetNuke install where the skin will be put in use. At step nine of this process, we package it so that it can be uploaded and used in any DotNetNuke install.

In the following chapters, we'll be going through each of these phases together, finishing off a skin that you can call your own.

What You Can Do With Skinning

Many wonder what exactly is possible with DotNetNuke's skinning engine while considering it as a viable option for their needs. As stated at the beginning of this chapter, the look and feel of a website is a big sticking point for people. The skinning engine of DotNetNuke is very flexible. It allows webmasters to have multiple looks and feels for their websites as desired by just changing the skins instead of redesigning the site content and layout. Instead of asking what it can do, a more productive question would be what it can't do.

The most confining factor will be your imagination. Besides that, the most challenging part of the skin to customize is the menu, and we will cover that in detail in a chapter by itself. All other roadblocks from there is your skill in getting HTML and CSS defined just right, and that just takes patience and some experience. Rest assured, with very few exceptions, you can get your DotNetNuke portal to look just as you envision!

Summary

We took a step back and looked at skinning overall here. You know what skinning is and what skins are made of. You are aware that DotNetNuke comes with at least one useful skin. You know that the sky is the limit as far as what you can do, and you know the scope of the process of skinning. You are now ready to jump right in and create your first skin!

2
Creating Your First Skin

The thought of creating your first skin may be intimidating. You may believe that there are steps that will have to be done just right or there's no point even getting started. The fact is that once you understand some simple concepts, skinning is relatively easy. Ultimately, you will need to know your HTML and CSS markup and styling, but that is common in any type of web design you would do anywhere. This chapter is geared toward those who have never created a skin, and it will get you over any anxiety you thought you had about creating a skin.

Choosing an Editor

If this is your first skin, you really should be thinking about what editor you will be using. If you don't already have an editor or the development environment for other coding you may be working with, the immediate choice that may come to mind is Microsoft Notepad, but there's no need to put yourself through that type of abuse.

As we're working with Microsoft technologies while working with DotNetNuke, the natural choice will be Microsoft Visual Web Developer (VWD) which is free. There are other choices for editors here, but VWD will be the one used by most in this context, so we'll move on with it in our examples. If you are using Microsoft's Visual Studio .NET (Microsoft's premier development environment), you will notice that the screens and menus are virtually the same.

Installing Visual Web Developer

Before we can do anything, we'll need VWD installed. If you have already installed VWD, feel free to skip this section. These are the steps for getting VWD installed:

1. Be sure you have version 2.0 of the .net framework. This can be downloaded from `http://www.asp.net` or with Windows Updates.

2. Download the VWD install file from `http://www.asp.net` from the **Downloads** section. The file will be about three megabytes in size.

3. Once on your local drive, double-click on the file to run the installation. You will encounter several common wizard screens. One wizard screen to note in particular is for installing SQL Server 2005 Express Edition. If you do not already have a version of SQL Server 2005 installed, be sure to select to install this. DotNetNuke will have to have an edition of this to run off for its data store.

   This is a screen shot of the recommended installation options to choose.

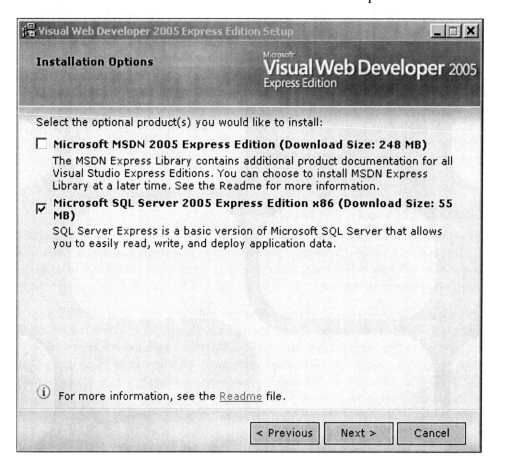

4. Stepping through the wizard, you will start the installation. The installation process may take a while depending upon what options you chose. For example, if you chose to install the MSDN library (documentation & help files), it will take much longer. It will only download the items it needs.

5. At the end of the installation, it will prompt you to register the software. If you do not register VWD within thirty days, it will stop working.

 If you encounter problems in the installation of VWD, you can find additional assistance at the `http://forums.asp.net/` discussion website.

Installing the DotNetNuke Starter Kits

Even though we now have VWD and SQL Server, we'll need the DotNetNuke files to set up before we can start skinning portals. Do so by using the following steps:

1. Navigate to `http://www.dotnetnuke.com`.

2. If you haven't already registered on this site, do so now.

3. If you are not already logged in, do so now.

4. Click on **Downloads** and download the latest version of the starter kit.

5. Right-click on the zip file you downloaded and extract the contents.

6. Double-click on the vscontent file that was extracted. This will start the **Visual Studio Content Installer**. Select all the components, and click **Next**.

7. Click **Finish** to install the starter kit. There are a few components that will be installed. See that in the next screenshot one of the components did not get installed. This is fine as long as the first one, **DotNetNuke Web Application** (the one we'll be using) installed successfully.

The following is what you should see so far:

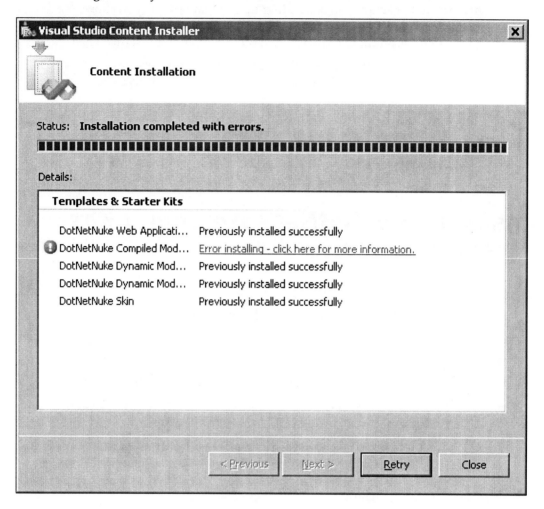

 If you encounter problems in the installation of the DotNetNuke starter kits, you can find additional assistance at the http://www.dotnetnuke.com/ website by clicking on the **Forums** link and then drilling-down to the **Install It!** link.

Setting Up Your Development Environment

In almost any programming project, you will have two environments: the development environment and the post-deployed environment. While skinning, this is no different. Most likely, you will have a local computer where you work on your skin. When you are done with it and are ready to package and deploy it, it will be installed on the target or live DotNetNuke website which will be your post-deployed environment.

To set up our development environment, fire up VWD. We'll now create a new DotNetNuke install:

1. Click on **File**, and then click **New Web Site**.
2. A dialog box appears. Click on **DotNetNuke Web Application Framework**.
3. For **Location**, pick **File System** (should be the default item), then type the following location beside it: **C:\DotNetNukeSkinning**.

This is the screenshot of what you should see so far:

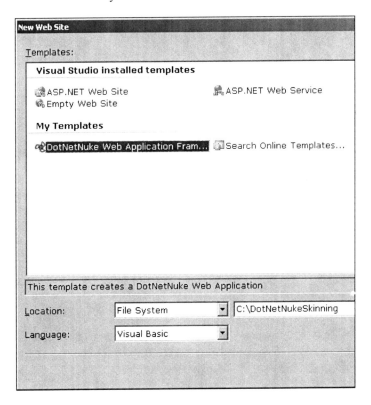

1. Click **OK**. It will take a few moments to copy over all the needed web files.

2. You will then be presented with a welcome screen. As the welcome page directs, press *Ctrl* plus *F5* to run your DotNetNuke application.

3. After a few moments, a DotNetNuke install should open in a web browser. If you are presented with the following message, right-click on the information bar at the top and enable the intranet settings in the Internet Explorer.

   This is what you should see at this point:

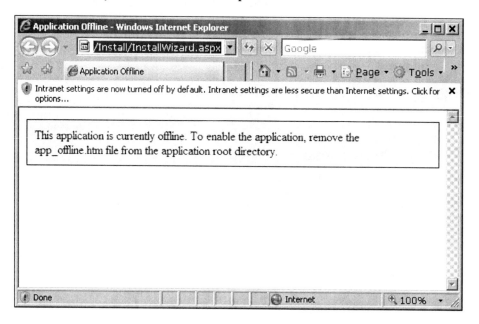

4. You are presented with a choice of installation methods. Select **Auto and** then select **Next**.

5. You should then see a web page with a log of installation of the application. Click on the link at the bottom that says **Click Here To Access Your Portal**.

If you encounter problems in the installation of the DotNetNuke, you can find additional assistance at the http://www.dotnetnuke.com/ website by clicking on the **Forums** link and then drilling-down to the **Install It!** link.

6. Congratulations! You now have DotNetNuke up and running. Click **Login** in the upper-right corner of the screen with the username as **host** and a password as **dnnhost**.

7. You should be on the **Home** page with several modules on it. To make the home page easier to work with, delete all the modules on it, and add a blank **Text/HTML** module. (In case you have never deleted a module from a page before, you will find the **delete** menu item if you hover over the downward-pointing triangles to the left of each of the titles.)

> Depending on the version of DNN you downloaded, you may experience a system message from DotNetNuke on the Home page titled **Insecure account details**. Although changing the default password as it instructs is always a good idea, it is not necessary on a development computer or a non-production implementation of DotNetNuke. However, if you don't want it to nag you about it go ahead and change it.

This is our DotNetNuke portal that we will use to test the skins we will create. Move back over to VWD. Close the welcome page.

As stated in Chapter 1, the skins for DotNetNuke will be found in `~\Portals\_default\Skins\`. Go to that directory now as shown here:

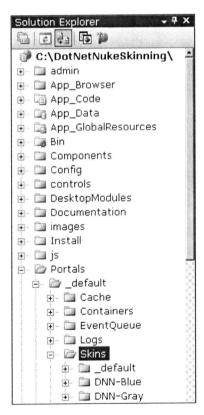

Congratulations! You have now set up your development environment, and we are now ready for skinning.

Creating Your First Skin

We will now create a skin and record time. You may be impressed by how fast and easy it is for you to create a skin.

 Remember when we downloaded the starter kits from `DotNetNuke.com`? One template is for creating a skin. As of the time of this writing, the current download's template will produce a skin that looks just like the default skin. If this is what you're looking for, you can achieve the same result by copying the `DNN-Blue` folder and renaming it to something else. Rather than doing this, however, we are starting from scratch.

1. Create a folder in your development environment. Name it as **FirstSkin**. In VWD, to create a new folder, right-click on the folder you want to create it in—in this case **Skins**—and select **New Folder**.

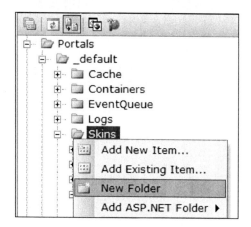

2. Next, create an htm file inside the FirstSkin folder called **Skin.htm**. Use the **File** menu to create a **New File**. This will bring up a dialog box where you will pick what type of file you wish to create. Pick **HTML Page** and name the file as **Skin.htm**.

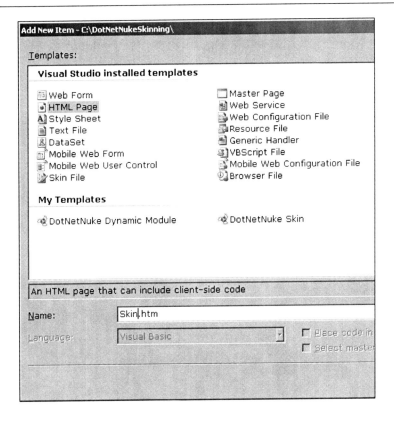

3.   Now, open our new **Skin.htm** file.

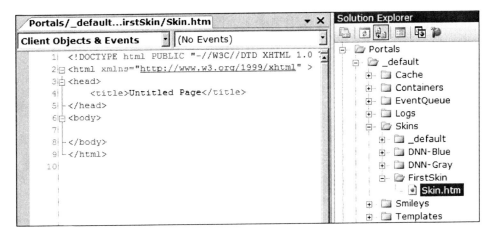

4. A typical htm document will have tags like `<html>`, `<head>`, and `<body>`. A DotNetNuke skin has none of these. Delete any content so you have clean slate to start from.

5. Once we have a blank htm page to work from, type in the following and save:

```
[LOGIN]
[MENU]
<div id="ContentPane" runat="server"></div>
```

6. Go to the **Skins** menu item on your **Admin** menu.

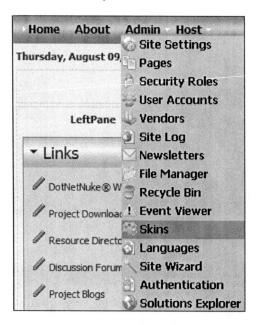

7. You will now see two drop-down boxes, one for **Skins** and one for **Containers**. In the drop-down for **Skins**, pick the skin you have created. You should see something like this:

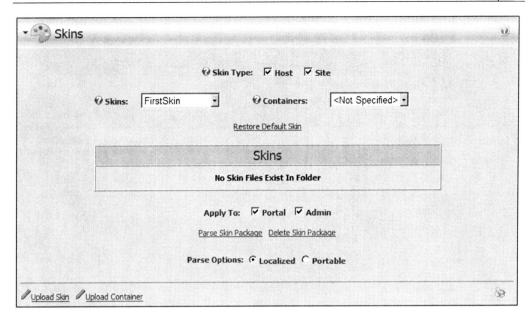

8. Click on the link in the lower-middle portion of the screen that says **Parse Skin Package**. You should see your skin now:

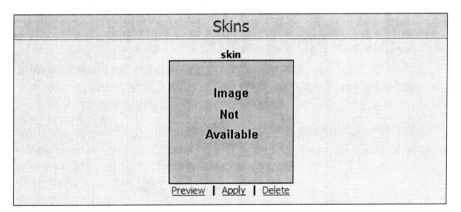

9. Now that our skin has been parsed, let's apply it to our current DotNetNuke portal by clicking on the **Apply** link.

 Keep in mind that we only have one pane, the **ContentPane**. If this was a live site with modules on other panes, the positions may have been changed.

10. Now, go to the home page by clicking on your menu bar at the top.

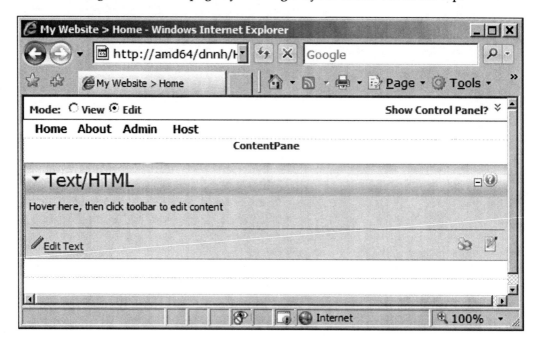

What Do We Have Here?

I know what you're thinking: This has got to be the world's simplest DotNetNuke skin. And you're right. You may not be rushing to install this skin on your production portals, but you have created your very first operational skin!

Let's go over what just happened, from creating our skin to seeing it in action. Skins start out as a simple HTML file. Just as with any website, an HTML file will have some degree of markup. Of course, we have not added much markup to our skin yet.

If you're wondering from where DotNetNuke gets all the HTML structure such as the `html`, `head`, and `body` tags, take a look at `Default.aspx` in the root of your DNN install. This is the page used essentially every time a page is served up. You can look in that file and find an ASP. NET element called `SkinPlaceHolder`. This is where our skin will be injected into each DotNetNuke page. Everything before and after this place holder is what will be served to any DNN page request no matter what skin is applied.

The code we entered for our skin is:

```
[LOGIN]
[MENU]
<div id="ContentPane" runat="server"></div>
```

Of the code we typed, [LOGIN] and [MENU] are special keywords to DotNetNuke, called **tokens**. The [Login] token will turn into the login link you're used to seeing and the [Menu] token will serve as our DotNetNuke menu. Adding the [login] token will ensure that we're not locked out of our portal after applying this skin. The <div> tag we added will be a simple ContentPane for now.

> Notice the two attributes we added to this <div> tag—id and runat.
> These are attributes required by ASP.NET. The id is a unique identifier in
> the page and the value given to it (ContentPane) is recognized as name by
> DotNetNuke. The runat attribute tells the ASP.NET engine that it needs
> to be processed by it.

Why Parse?

Recall when we clicked on a link to parse our skin. What DotNetNuke does at this point is take our HTM file and replace those tokens with ASP.NET user controls that have been predefined in DotNetNuke. (Tokens are the representations of SkinObjects, which will be covered in thorough detail in Chapter 5.) At the end of this parsing process, the result is an ASCX file that becomes the real skin file, which is loaded into the Default.aspx at the runtime event of a page request.

Anytime after parsing the skin for the first time, you may go in and look at the ASCX file with a text editor, and even modify and see immediate changes without doing a parse. As tempting as editing the ASCX file may be (especially if you're an ASP.NET developer and understand editing ASCX files), you really should not be doing that. This ASCX file is regenerated and is replaced each time a HTM skin file is re-parsed. We will also want to create our skins in a way that would be compatible with the future versions of DotNetNuke. Starting off with an HTM skin file puts us on the path to achieve this goal.

Finishing Touches

The next thing you will want to do is add more tokens and a little HTML to make yourself a little more proud of your DNN skin. To do this, go back to your HTM file and add two or three items from the list of tokens shown as follows:

```
[LOGO]
[BANNER]
[SEARCH]
[LANGUAGE]
[CURRENTDATE]
[BREADCRUMB]
[USER]
[COPYRIGHT]
[TERMS]
[PRIVACY]
[DOTNETNUKE]
```

 For a complete list of all DotNetNuke tokens, please refer to the **DotNetNuke Skinning Guide** document by **Shaun Walker**. You can download it from `http://www.dotnetnuke.com/LinkClick.aspx?fileticket=2ptHepzmuFA%3d&tabid=478&mid=857`.

Now add in some HTML. You may want to add in a few `<hr/>` (horizontal rule) or `<br/>` (vertical break) tags to separate things out.

When you make changes and want to see them, remember to go to the **Admin** menu and then to the **Skins** page and re-parse the skin, then go to the **Home** page to see the changes.

Summary

The title for this chapter was *Creating Your First Skin* and that's exactly what we did. There are many reasons why you couldn't or wouldn't use this skin for a live site. Of course any website needs a good design, and some graphics, but if you've managed a DNN site, before you know you'll need some more panes and some precise positioning. We'll start tackling these topics in the next few pages.

3
Page Layout

In the last chapter, we created a skin. It worked and was functional, but that was it. It lacked layout and structure. You should now understand how easy it is to get a base skin up and running. Now it is time to give it some much needed structure!

Page Design and Layout

Think of a DotNetNuke site and imagine it without any modules or skin objects in it. What you have is page design and the layout of that site. It's the part that is generally constant from page to page. It includes how things are laid out and is what one would call the look of the site. Page design is the heart and soul of any DotNetNuke skin.

Take a look at the next figure. This is an example of a typical web page layout. It has a banner at the top followed by some type of menu to navigate through the site. Each site will have content which will fit into pre-arranged panes. At the bottom you have a footer which will have more links, disclaimers, and other pertinent small print.

The DotNetNuke skin we'll be building in this book will loosely follow this type of structure since it is used for most purposes. As you work through the steps in the book, feel free to customize it to your needs.

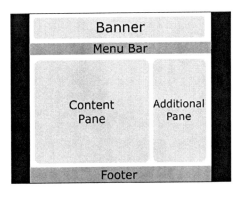

How to Position

The next step we need to take in constructing our skin is to position these components of our page. There are essentially two ways to design and structure a web page/site:

1. With HTML tables
2. With CSS positioning

The default DotNetNuke skin utilizes HTML tables to achieve its traditional layout. Creating a layout in HTML is easy to understand and implement by most people.

The following is a simplified example of how you might achieve the above layout:

```
<table>
  <tr>
    <td>Banner</td>
  </tr>
  <tr>
    <td>Menu Bar</td>
  </tr>
  <tr>
    <td>
      <!-- nested table for positioning our panes -->
      <table>
        <tr>
          <td>
            Content Pane
          </td>
          <td>
            Additional Pane
          </td>
        </tr>
      </table>
    </td>
  </tr>
  <tr>
    <td>Footer</td>
  </tr>
</table>
```

There are lots of `<tr>` and `<td>` tags in there. You may notice how important the indention is to this type of approach. If you don't indent, how will you know what closing tag goes with the opening tag? Keep in mind that this is a simplified version of what it would really be.

The <table> tag was not intended to be used for positioning and structure of web pages. They were meant to be used to hold the tables of information. As HTML evolved, designers of these web standards sought the means to separate the content from presentation or appearance of the content. CSS was a means to this goal.

CSS positioning, also known as "standards based design" is a logical choice if you have already taken the time to learn it. Most who are beginners at DotNetNuke skinning may not be experts at Cascading Style Sheets positioning. The following is an example of what the markup would look like if CSS positioning is used:

```
<div id="doc" class="MainContainer">
  <div id="Banner">
    Banner
  </div>
  <div id="Menu">
    Menu
  </div>
  <div id="Panes">
    <div id="ContentPane">
      Content Pane
    </div>
    <div class="RightPane">
      Right Pane
    </div>
  </div>
  <div id="Footer">
    Footer
  </div>
</div>
```

Note that there is no CSS defined here. The style is typically defined in a separate file with an extension of CSS. Most of the complexity is found in this CSS file where you would define how each of these <div> elements would be positioned and sized.

Even though you use HTML table-based design here, you will probably still have a CSS file that will define some degree of styling for that table but mostly other components of your page. There is no way of getting around it; you will have both HTML and CSS in your DNN skins.

CSS positioning is not a rocket science, but it is more of a challenge to pick up than tables-based design. This is why we'll be using mostly tables-based design in this book. However, if you happen to be fluent in the CSS design, you'll have no problem translating some of the proposed table designs into CSS design. The skinning concepts presented in this book will apply no matter which route you choose.

The Challenge that Lies Ahead

There are two main challenges that lie ahead—knowledge and skill in HTML and CSS—for any web design. If you're a DotNetNuke enthusiast and don't have a background in web development, this may be a huge hurdle to get over. Unfortunately, for such circumstance, this is not a book on HTML or CSS. You may find the need to supplement this material with some that covers these topics well. Even those who do have a solid background in HTML and CSS may feel challenged from time to time when it comes down to fine-tuning and getting things just right.

You will need to get your layout to work like the same in all the browsers available. If you're concerned about how your skin will appear in other browsers other than the one you use, it would be a prudent idea to download and install the four or five top used browsers:

- Internet Explorer
- Firefox
- Safari
- Opera
- Netscape

Browser Caching

Before moving on with editing our skin, we should disable caching in the web browser we're using so that we're able to see the changes right after we save them. If you don't do this, you may wonder why a change isn't working or think you didn't enter correct syntax even if you did.

1. In the **Internet Explorer**, go to the **Tools** menu, and choose **Internet Options**.

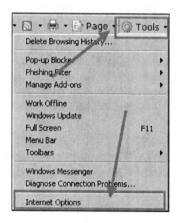

2. Click on the **Settings** button.

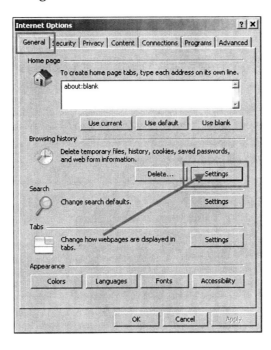

3. Choose the option: **Every time I visit the webpage**.

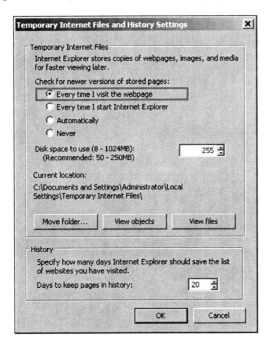

Moving On with Our Skin

It's time to take our simplistic skin and put in some sensible structure and layout. We'll get this all kick-started with VWD's designer tools.

1. Go to the code for the HTM file. Delete all the code in the file. We'll need to start from a clean slate.

2. Click on the **Design** button at the bottom of the coding window of your HTM file. This will take you from editing your HTM file with code/markup to editing it with a visual designer. We'll use VWD's designer here to do as much grunt work as possible to help us.

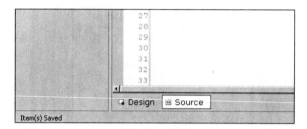

3. From the menu bar at the top, click on **Layout**, and then click **Insert Table**.

4. Insert a **Custom** table having **1** row and **1** column with a **Width** and **Height** of **100%**. See the following screenshot. This will be our all-inclusive table that will hold all other content in our skin.

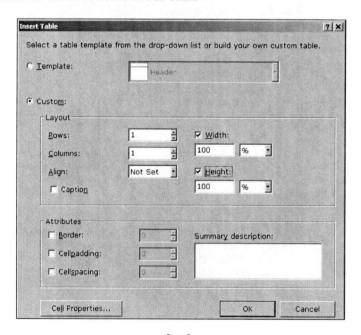

5. Click **OK**. This should give us a border that goes to the edges of our skin. We'll create and insert virtually everything in this boundary from now on, so click inside it and make sure you have a blinking cursor.

6. Insert another table by going to the menu bar just as we did above. This time we'll create a **5** row, **1** column table that will take up **800** pixels. While this dialog box is open, change the **Align** drop-down to **Center**.

7. You should now see your five row table in the designer. The first row will be used for the DNN control panel. Go to that row and type in [CONTROLPANEL] to remind us what will go in there.

8. In the second row, we'll create three tables. They will not be nested, but be sure you stay in this second row we're now on to create all three. Create the first one as a **1** row, **2** column table that takes up the **100%** **Width**. In the first column, type [LOGO]. In the second column, type [BANNER].

9. Again, in the second row but outside and after the one we just created, create the second of the three tables. This will be just like that last one we created; it will have 1 row and 2 columns and will take up 100% width. In the first column type [NAV]. In the second column, type [SEARCH] [LANGUAGE].

10. Staying in this second row, create the last of the three tables. This one will have **1** row, but **3** columns. It will also take up **100%** of the **Width** of its parent's table of **800** pixels. In column one, type [CURRENTDATE]. In column two, type [BREADCRUMB]. In column three, type [USER] and [LOGIN] with a space between them.

11. Going now to the third row, insert only one table, but make it to be of **3** rows and **3** columns and with a **Width** of **100%** and a **Height** of **100%**. This table will hold our panes. Go to the top-center cell in the newly created table and type [TOPPANE]. Go to the second row and type [LEFTPANE] in the left cell, [CONTENTPANE] in the center cell, and [RIGHTPANE] in the right cell. On the bottom row in the center cell, type [BOTTOMPANE].

12. In the fourth row, add a **1** row, **1** column table with a **Width** of **100%**. Inside it, type [COPYRIGHT], [TERMS], [PRIVACY] with a space in between them.

13. In the fifth row, add a **1** row, **1** column table with a **100%** **Width** and type [DOTNETNUKE] inside.

Congratulations! You just created the whole table structure for your skin.

Just as we went from the source view of our HTM file to the designer before, we'll need to switch back now to the source view. Before we parse and view this skin, we need to make several modifications to our code to make it usable.

1. One thing the VWD designer does while creating tables, as it just did, is that it makes the table cells (or `<td>`'s) have a width of 100 pixels. Let's change this. Look in our HTM file's markup code for our portion of a `<td>` tag that says `style="width: 100px"` (do not confuse this with 100%). Press *Ctrl* plus *H* to bring up the **find and replace** dialog box. The **Replace With** box should have nothing in it. See the following figure. Now, click on **Replace All**.

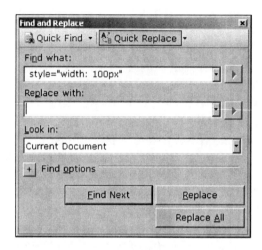

2. For some of the `<td>` tags we have, we'll need to go in and set the alignment up to be appropriate to what we expect. For example, typically the menu and the search skin objects are beside each other or on the same table row. If you don't set the alignment in a table cell, it will justify it to the left by default. This is okay for the menu in DNN. This is what we expect. But for the search box, if we don't align its containing `<td>` to the right, then it will look as if the search bar is floating in the middle of the page. Find the `<td>` tag that contains the `[SEARCH]` and `[LANGUAGE]` tokens and create an attribute called `align` and set its value to `"right"` (you should always include attribute values in double-quotes for adhering to the XHMTL standard). After typing it in, be sure to select the attribute, value, and the space before it (see the following code).

```
<table style="width: 100%">
    <tr>
        <td>
            [NAV]</td>
        <td align="right">
            [SEARCH][LANGUAGE]</td>
    </tr>
</table>
```

3. The reason why we select what we just typed is that we need to copy and paste it. Do so now for the <td> containing [USER] and [LOGIN].

4. Some other <td>'s in our skin need to be aligned as well, but with their attribute set to center (take advantage of copy-paste again):

    ○   All the <td>'s containing the panes: [TOPPANE], [LEFTPANE], [CONTENTPANE], & [RIGHTPANE].

    ○   The <td> containing the [BREADCRUMB] token.

    ○   The <td> that contains the [COPYRIGHT], [TEMRS], and [PRIVACY] tokens.

    ○   The <td> that contains the [DOTNETNUKE] token.

5. As HTML table cells align content to the left by default, they also vertically align content to the middle, not to the top. The panes which will hold the module content will not look quite right like this. Go into these <td>'s and add the attribute valign="top" to each of them.

6. We'll have to do something different with [CONTROLPANEL] as it is not really a DNN token. Here we just typed that in to know where the control panel would be placed. DNN will automatically insert a control panel at the top of our skin. However, if you want to force it to be in a specific place, we can do two things to make it so:

    ○   Give an html containing tag such as a <div>, or a <td> in this case

    ○   Add an attribute called runat with the value of server.

    ```
    <td id="ControlPanel" runat="server">[CONTROLPANEL]</td>
    ```

7. After you add the id and runat attributes, take out the [CONTROLPANEL] text. We do not need it anymore and it will only get in the way.

8. The text we used for the panes are not DNN tokens as well. We'll need to change these too. Again, add in id and runat attributes to those five containing <td> tags. Then remove the text the way we did with the [ControlPanel]. A sample of what your code should look like is shown at the end of these steps:

9. In the designer when we created the table for the content pane, we created a 3 by 3 table. The top and bottom panes should span the same three columns that the left, center, and right panes take up. Take out the excess <td>'s around the [TopPane] and the [BottomPane] by deleting the empty <td> tags (<td></td>). For example, your code should go from looking like the following code to the one that's shown after it:

```
<tr>
    <td></td>
    <td align="center" valign="top"
     id="TopPane" runat="server"></td>
    <td></td>
</tr>
```

The following is what your code should look like:

```
<tr>
  <td align="center" valign="top"
      id="TopPane" runat="server"></td>
</tr>
```

 A skin can have as many panes as you'd like. You can add more by adding them with an id that ends with Pane as we did here. Creating panes like this, as opposed to adding them as tokens, allows us to make the table details into panes.

Be sure to do this not only for the [TopPane] row, but also for the [BottomPane].

10. Now, these pane rows won't look quite right because they still would not span the width of the three panes in the middle, so now we need to add an attribute called colspan and set its value to three (colspan="3").

```
<tr>
  <td align="center" valign="top"
      id="TopPane" runat="server"
        colspan="3">
  </td>
</tr>
```

Again, be sure to do this for the [BottomPane] containing <td> as well.

Now go to your skin administrative page and parse your skin once again, then click **Home** to go back.

Your menus may be transparent and a little difficult to navigate because of it. Don't be concerned at this point. Once we add some style, this will be taken care of.

You should see something like this:

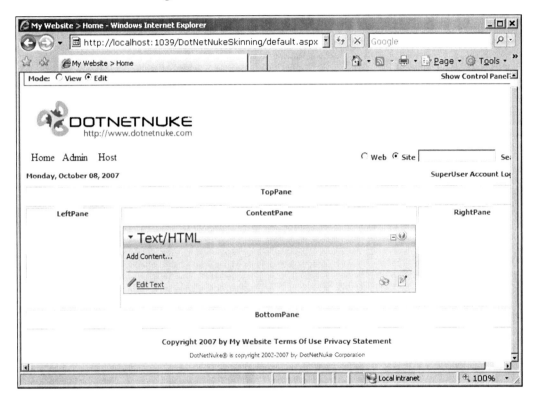

Summary

We have taken the simplistic skin and gave it some structure and layout. At this point, it actually looks like a skin. The next logical step is to give this skin some style which we'll do in the next chapter.

4
Adding Style

Our skin desperately needs some style. Style is a grouping of settings that define how something should look. The way we implement style is through cascading style sheets. It could be to make a pane, skin object, or to make a general font of our skin be a certain color, size, have a picture behind it, or have a certain margin. This is what our skin lacks now as a whole.

A CSS Refresher

There are things you should know about CSS before jumping in and inserting style into your skin. We should touch on some of these CSS basics before we jump in too fast. If you don't understand the basics of CSS before continuing, going through the rest of this book may become a frustration.

Cascading style sheets is a technology to supplement HTML to define how the content in HTML should look. It does not replace HTML. CSS needs a way to hook into your content and it needs the HTML tags to do this. And HTML is just plain, limited as to what it can define for looks and positioning.

There are three locations where you can store the style:

1. **Inline**, which is inside an attribute called `style` within an HTML tag. Example:

   ```
   <td style="color:red;">here is some red text</td>
   ```

   You can add the `style` attribute to virtually any HTML tag and define style. In this example, the text inside this table cell would be red in color.

2. **In style tags**, which have the scope of the whole HTML document. Example:

   ```
   <style>
       td {color:red;}
   </style>
   ```

Although the style tags are typically in the head section of the HTML, you could in fact put them anywhere in the HTML document. This is important in our case when DotNetNuke has already created the head section of the HTML stream to be sent to the browser. By the time our skin gets injected into the DNN page, we are well inside the body section of the HTML document. In this last example, the default font color for the table details of this skin will be red.

3. **A separate CSS file**, which typically affects the whole site, or in this case our skin. For example, in an HTML document, you would place something like the following:

```
<link rel="stylesheet" type="text/css" href="something.css">
```

It then links to the style in a separate CSS file:

```
<style>
    td {color:red;}
</style>
```

Cascading Rules

The style-defined in style tags will override the style defined in a separate file. And the style-defined inline will override or cascade those in style tags and those in a separate CSS file. You don't have to wonder where the name *cascade* comes from in cascading style sheets!

If certain styles only apply to a particular HTML element, then you would use inline style. If style applies to more than one element or you want to be prepared for using that style for another element on a particular page, you would use the style tags. If used site-wide, or in our case, skin-wide (as skins are applied typically to a whole DNN site), you should use the CSS files.

 Defining style in CSS files makes for faster page loading times because browsers will cache these separate files, according to your browser's cache settings.

Seeing Style in Action

For those of you who haven't worked much with CSS, it may help to see the real world examples of how all this works. If you have, you may still want to see a good example of how it all fits into DotNetNuke. Let's take a look:

1. Go to the **Admin** menu and then go to **Skins**.
2. Change the skin to DNN-Blue.

3. Click **Apply** on the first of the four skins displayed.

4. Click on **Home**.

5. You should see the familiar DotNetNuke skin in action here. Right-click on a blank spot on the page. This should bring up a shortcut menu. Select **View Source**. (see the following screenshot)

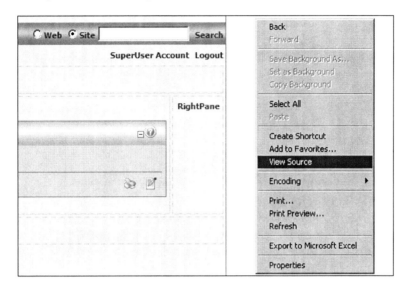

6. You should now be looking at a fairly large HTML document inside Notepad or some other text editor. This is what was sent to and rendered in the browser. Find some of the style definitions in the head section of the document. You may need to use your horizontal scrollbar or turn wordwrap on. Feel free to add carriage returns in this document. It will not affect your skin or DotNetNuke. You should see something like this amidst the HTML document:

```
<style id="StylePlaceholder" type="text/css"></style>

<link id="_DotNetNukeSkinning_Portals__default_" rel="stylesheet"
type="text/css" href="/DotNetNukeSkinning/Portals/_default/
default.css" />

<link id="_DotNetNukeSkinning_Portals__default_Skins_dnn_blue_"
rel="stylesheet" type="text/css" href="/DotNetNukeSkinning/
Portals/_default/Skins/dnn-blue/skin.css" />

<link id="_DotNetNukeSkinning_Portals__default_Containers_DNN_
Blue_" rel="stylesheet" type="text/css" href="/DotNetNukeSkinning/
Portals/_default/Containers/DNN-Blue/container.css" />

<link id="_DotNetNukeSkinning_Portals_0_" rel="stylesheet"
type="text/css" href="/DotNetNukeSkinning/Portals/0/portal.css" />
```

Carriage returns (vertical spaces) have been added to make the preceding code more readable.

By looking at the `href` attributes in the preceding code, you can find the CSS files in our DNN project in Visual Web Developer. Open one or two of them up and look at the defined style.

You can see that DotNetNuke relies heavily on CSS files to make up its design. Look up in the code we got by going to **View Source** and you will find some inline style defined. So, perform a search by pressing *Ctrl* plus *F* for the text **style=**. Also notice the attributes called `class` sprinkled throughout the document. These class names will reference the style defined in the linked CSS files.

A Portal's CSS in Site Settings

For someone who is running a DotNetNuke site, you can always go into and override what the programmer or skinner defined in these CSS files. For each DotNetNuke portal, you may have noticed that in the **Site Settings** item on the **Admin** menu, at the bottom there is a place to define style. See the following figure:

```
Stylesheet Editor

/* ====================================
   CSS STYLES FOR DotNetNuke
   ====================================
*/


/* PAGE BACKGROUND */
/* background color for the header at the top of the page  */
.HeadBg {
}

/* background color for the content part of the pages */
Body
{
}

.ControlPanel {
}
```

Save Style Sheet   Restore Default Style Sheet

Update

If you look in the ~\Portals_default directory, you will find two CSS files. The file portal.css is used as a CSS template to populate this textbox. It gives the blank defined CSS classes for you to modify. If you click on the **Restore Default Style Sheet** link, it will read in this CSS file again and use its contents to reset this. If you were to make changes, it saves the contents to a file called portal.css into the root of your portal. This is one of the CSS files we saw referenced when we opened **View Source**.

More Style to Cascade

DotNetNuke helps you define style at different levels. To accomplish this, it will inject declarations for more CSS files in this order as you saw in the **View Source** document:

1. ~/Portals/_default/default.css—This file contains some default styles for the control panel, skin objects, and other items. When no style is defined anywhere else, this file provides a base style definition.

2. Your skin.css file—If you have a CSS file in your skin directory called skin.css, it will be used. This is where the most, if not all, of the style for your skin will be defined.

3   The default container.css file—This is where the style for the containers is. We will talk more about this in the chapter covering containers.

4. A portal.css file that is in the root of your portal directory mentioned above.

Keep in mind that even if the style is defined at one level, it can and is being overridden by another CSS file lower on the list (in the order above). For example, the person who installed DotNetNuke (a host-level or a super user) could go in and change the default.css file which would affect all the portals under that DNN install. Then we (as skinners) could create a skin and container, which would be the skin.css and container.css (we'll create our container.css file in the chapter on containers). These styles would override the default styles the host puts in. If the admin of a DotNetNuke site were to go into the site settings and insert some more styles, then our skin's style is overridden.

Back to Our Skin

Now, we will create our CSS file, then we'll define our style there and link it in our HTM file with the class attributes.

1. In the **Solution Explorer** window within VWD, right-click on **FirstSkin** and select **Add New Item…**.

2. You'll be provided with a list of file types to choose from. Select the **Style Sheet** item and name the file as **Skin**.

3. Keep both the HTM and the CSS file open in VWD, but go to the HTM file.

4. Now that our CSS file is created, let's start setting up our classes in the HTM and CSS files.

5. The first line of HTML code defines a table which serves as a container for everything else in the skin. We'll refer to this as `PageContainer`. Add the `class` attribute and set its value to `PageContainer`. (see the following screenshot)

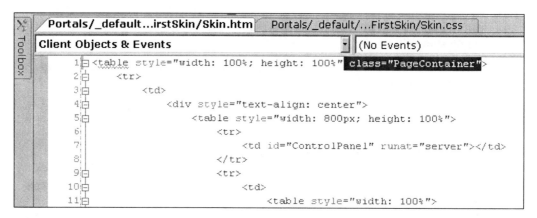

 It doesn't matter what we call CSS classes as long as we give them a name and that they are somewhat meaningful to use.

6. Now, if you remember from the last chapter, the designer helped us and inserted some style for us, `style="width: 100%; height: 100%"`. This is there to make sure that this table takes up all the available space as an all-encompassing container, which is what we want. However, it would be best to move this style over to our CSS file we just created. We just added the class attribute in the HTM file, now let's create it over in our CSS file.

```
Portals/_default...irstSkin/Skin.htm    Portals/_default/...FirstSkin/Skin.css
 1    .PageContainer {
 2        width: 100%;
 3        height: 100%;
 4    }
 5
 6
 7
 8
 9
10
```

7. While we're here, let's add a background color to this style so that the sides become a darker color than that of the main content in the center. This is done in web design to focus the web visitor's attention on the content. Add the following after the `height`:

```
Background-color: #888888;
```

8. Now go back to the HTM document and take out the whole style attribute.

9. If we were to parse this skin right now, virtually all of our skin would have this dark color as a background, which is not what we want. We just want it on the sides. It's time to give our five-row content table in the middle a background of white. Go to your HTM file and find the table element that has a `style` attribute which sets the `width` to `800px`. Let's give it a `class` name of `ContentContainer`.

```
1  <table class="PageContainer">
2      <tr>
3          <td>
4              <div style="text-align: center">
5                  <table style="width: 800px; height: 100%" class="ContentContainer">
6                      <tr>
```

10. Now take out the whole style attribute there.

11. Create the class in the CSS file and add the values that were set in the style attribute we just removed and add in a background color of white (you can either spell out white or use its hexadecimal value of `#ffffff`):

```
ContentContainer
{
    width: 800px;
    height: 100%;
    background-color: #ffffff;
}
```

12. Parse and view the changes in your skin to see the result.

13. As you can see, it does look better but it has far too much white in the middle and all the skin objects just seem to float in the random locations. If we add in a little contrast, it will help this significantly. Find the table that contains the menu, the search, and the language skin objects. Create a `class` attribute and call it `MenuContainer`.

14. Create a style definition in the CSS file and set the background color:

```
MenuContainer
{
     background-color: #dddddd;
}
```

15. Notice that the table in the HTM file has a `style` attribute that sets the `width`. Let's take this out and move it to the CSS file.

```
MenuContainer
{
     background-color: #dddddd;
     width: 100%;
}
```

16. Let's now do the same thing we've done for the menu table to the table which contains the `Copyright`, `Terms`, and `Privacy` links. We'll call its class as `FooterContainer`.

```
FooterContainer
{
     background-color: #dddddd;
     width: 100%;
}
```

17. Go to the **Skin Administrative** page, then parse and apply our skin. Go back **Home** to take a look at what we have got so far.

A Spacing Problem

Using Microsoft's Internet Explorer, you may have noticed that some of our HTML table cells are taking up more space than what we'd like. For example, if you log out and have very little content in the content panes, as we do now, you'll notice that the banner floats around a bit. See the following figure:

An HTML table will automatically change the width and height of its cells depending on what content they hold in relation to the other cells. In this case, there isn't much taking up space in the content panes, leaving more for the cell that holds the banner. However, the space here is not wanted. We can fix this by setting the cell's height to a small value. But which cell do we modify? All these nested tables can make it hard to find where the extra padding is coming from. A trick you can use is adding an attribute to some of the tables—border="1" (but be sure to change it back shortly after). This will allow us to see the boundaries of the tables and the cells. If you do a bit of investigation, you may have zeroed in on the following <td> that's highlighted:

```
 9      <tr>
10          <td>
11              <table style="width: 100%;">
12                  <tr>
13                      <td>
14                          [LOGO] </td>
15                      <td>
16                          [BANNER] </td>
17                  </tr>
18              </table>
19              <table class="MenuContainer">
20                  <tr>
21                      <td>
22                          [NAV] </td>
23                      <td align="right">
24                          [SEARCH] [LANGUAGE] </td>
25                  </tr>
26              </table>
27              <table style="width: 100%">
28                  <tr>
29                      <td>
30                          [CURRENTDATE] </td>
31                      <td align="center">
32                          [BREADCRUMB] </td>
33                      <td align="right">
34                          [USER] [LOGIN] </td>
35                  </tr>
36              </table>
37          </td>
38      </tr>
```

We can either guess the exact height this cell should be based on the size of the banner (which can change based on what banner is used in the skin) and everything else, or we can set the height to the smallest value and let the browser enlarge it based on what's inside. Another decision to be made is to put the CSS style inline or in our CSS file. In this case as we won't be defining much other style for it or other cells like it, so let's just put it inline like this on that first `<td>` tag:

```
<td style="height:1px;">
```

We'll also need to apply this positioning to some of the other table cells? If you play around with sizing your browser you'll notice that the footer cells need it as well.

```
<tr>
    <td style="height:1px;">
        <table class="FooterContainer">
            <tr>
                <td align="center">
                    [COPYRIGHT] [TERMS] [PRIVACY]</td>
            </tr>
        </table>
    </td>
</tr>
<tr>
    <td align="center" style="height:1px;">
        [DOTNETNUKE]</td>
</tr>
```

Now, set the control panel's `<td>` to the same:

```
<td id="ControlPanel" runat="server" style="height:1px;"></td>
```

All these vertical gaps should be closed up now. Re-parse your skin to verify.

Browser Compatability

Once things start to shape up visually in your default browser, you should really fire up one or two other popular browsers to make sure things look consistent. Up to this point, we've been using the Internet Explorer.

If you haven't already done so, download Firefox by navigating to `http://www.mozilla.com/en-US/firefox/`. Save the file and run the installation to install it.

Let's view our skin in Firefox. You can simply go to your DNN site in the Internet Explorer and copy the web address, then paste it in Firefox, and then hit your enter key.

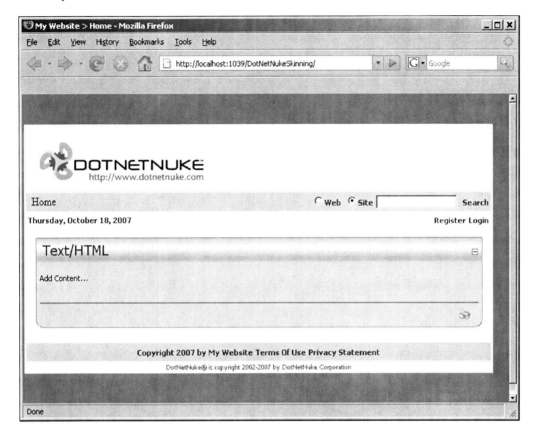

There are two things that come to light immediately:

1. Our main content table is not centered. It is justified to the left side of the screen.

2. The same content table is not stretching the whole height of the browser like the `PageContainer` is.

To tackle these two problems, let's go back to our HTM file and take a look at our first table's code:

```
<table class="PageContainer">
    <tr>
        <td align="center">
            <div style="text-align: center">
                <table class="ContentContainer" border="0">
```

There are two things we need to change to fix this. The first involves adding an `align` attribute with the value of `center`. Notice that the preceding code already has this in it. The next thing to do is to remove the `<div>` tag. Make sure you get the matching closing tag near the bottom of your HTM file. If you don't see the `<div>` tags, then don't worry about it. Save and re-parse. This takes care of the rendering problems inside Firefox.

Summary

There is more style we'll add throughout this book. Here, we added a CSS file and added some style our skin needed. We also went over some vital information in understanding how CSS works and cascades in DotNetNuke.

5

Configuring Skin Objects

With each chapter we have been shaping up our skin more and more. In the previous chapter, we gave our skin some style, but not much. Before we can add much more, we'll have to configure our skin objects properly so that the attributes and thus style can be set, among other things.

What are Skin Objects

We have been working with skin objects from the beginning. The banner, the menu, and the other pieces of a DotNetNuke site you're used to seeing are skin objects. Just like with modules, there are skin objects that come with DNN and there are ones you can download or purchase from other places.

The following are the default DNN skin objects with some descriptions:

Name	Token	Description
Logo	[LOGO]	This holds a graphics file which represents the entity or the topic your site is about. This is commonly referred to a banner, but don't confuse this with the DNN banner skin object listed next.
Banner	[BANNER]	This is a place holder for advertising banners.
Menu	[NAV]	This is the menu or navigational control of the site. In the past, the tokens [SOLPARTMENU] and [MENU] have been used.
Search	[SEARCH]	This allows users to search the content within your site, or now, with later versions of DNN, the web.
Language	[LANGUAGE]	On a multilingual DNN site, it allows the user to change his/her preferred language.

Name	Token	Description
Current Date	[CURRENTDATE]	This simply displays the current date based on the location of the web server.
Breadcrumb	[BREADCRUMB]	Lists out the hierarchical location of the page you're currently on.
Username	[USER]	This will display your username when you're logged in or **Register** when you're not. When it displays your username, it will link the user to their account settings. When it displays **Register**, it will link to a page where the user may register.
Login	[LOGIN]	Allows users to log in and log out.
Copyright	[COPYRIGHT]	Displays a simple copyright notice.
Terms of Use	[TERMS]	Links to a page where the terms of use are located.
Privacy Statement	[PRIVACY]	Links to a page where the privacy statement is mentioned.
DotNetNuke Copyright	[DOTNETNUKE]	Displays copyright information on DotNetNuke and links to its site.
Help	[HELP]	Displays the text **Help** as a link to the site's administrator.
Host Name	[HOSTNAME]	Displays a link to the host portal within the DNN install.
Tree View Menu	[TREEVIEWMENU]	Serves as a navigational menu with expandable and collapsible nodes. This is typically used on the left side of a DNN skin.
Links	[LINKS]	Displays a list of links to the parent and sibling levels of pages within the site. This makes it easier for search engines to index your site.

As you can see, some of these skin objects we are currently using and some we are not. Usually you do not see the help, host name, and links skin objects in action. They are not used in the default skins, but there's nothing to stop us from adding them to our skins.

What is There to Do with Skin Objects

Up to this point, we already know how to add skin objects to our skin. We've been adding the skin object tokens from Chapter 2. However, what we have not been able to do from the beginning is to customize these skin objects.

When our skin is parsed by DotNetNuke, it finds our tokens and compares them to a database table in its database to match them up with ASP.NET user controls (think of the packaged functionality). It then creates our skin as an ASCX file (which technically is another ASP.NET user control) and refers to the other ASCX files that are the skin objects. Let's see what this looks like:

1. In VWD, find your **FirstSkin** directory. You should see the HTM and the CSS file. We need to open the ASCX file. If you don't see the ASCX file, you need to refresh the directory by right-clicking on the **FirstSkin** folder and selecting **Refresh Folder**. Open the Skin.ascx file.

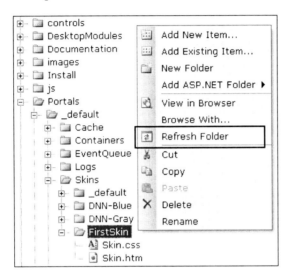

2. At the top of the ASCX file you will notice ASP.NET Register tags. Notice the TagName attribute in each of them. It is obvious that these are referencing each of the ASP.NET user controls in the DotNetNuke install directories for each of the skin objects. See the following screenshot:

```
1  <%@ Control language="vb" CodeBehind="~/admin/Skins/skin.vb" AutoEventWireup="false" Explic
2  <%@ Register TagPrefix="dnn" TagName="LOGO" Src="~/Admin/Skins/Logo.ascx" %>
3  <%@ Register TagPrefix="dnn" TagName="BANNER" Src="~/Admin/Skins/Banner.ascx" %>
4  <%@ Register TagPrefix="dnn" TagName="NAV" Src="~/Admin/Skins/Nav.ascx" %>
5  <%@ Register TagPrefix="dnn" TagName="SEARCH" Src="~/Admin/Skins/Search.ascx" %>
6  <%@ Register TagPrefix="dnn" TagName="LANGUAGE" Src="~/Admin/Skins/Language.ascx" %>
7  <%@ Register TagPrefix="dnn" TagName="CURRENTDATE" Src="~/Admin/Skins/CurrentDate.ascx" %>
8  <%@ Register TagPrefix="dnn" TagName="BREADCRUMB" Src="~/Admin/Skins/BreadCrumb.ascx" %>
9  <%@ Register TagPrefix="dnn" TagName="USER" Src="~/Admin/Skins/User.ascx" %>
10 <%@ Register TagPrefix="dnn" TagName="LOGIN" Src="~/Admin/Skins/Login.ascx" %>
11 <%@ Register TagPrefix="dnn" TagName="COPYRIGHT" Src="~/Admin/Skins/Copyright.ascx" %>
12 <%@ Register TagPrefix="dnn" TagName="TERMS" Src="~/Admin/Skins/Terms.ascx" %>
13 <%@ Register TagPrefix="dnn" TagName="PRIVACY" Src="~/Admin/Skins/Privacy.ascx" %>
14 <%@ Register TagPrefix="dnn" TagName="DOTNETNUKE" Src="~/Admin/Skins/DotNetNuke.ascx" %>
```

3. This isn't all. If you scroll down and look into the various places we put our tokens, you will see these replaced with the ASP.NET tags which reference those tags at the top.

 If you're not an ASP.NET developer, these tags may seem foreign to you. First of all, ASP.NET user controls are packaged, commonly reusable functionality you can drop on pages or other user controls. This is a two-step process as you just saw: 1. Register the control at the top. 2. Declare the control with the id and runat attributes which reference the TagPrefix and TagName declared in the Register tag at the top.

```
<table style="width: 100%;">
    <tr>
        <td>
            <dnn:LOGO runat="server" id="dnnLOGO" /></td>
        <td>
            <dnn:BANNER runat="server" id="dnnBANNER" /></td>
    </tr>
</table>
<table class="MenuContainer">
    <tr>
        <td>
            <dnn:NAV runat="server" id="dnnNAV" /></td>
        <td align="right">
            <dnn:SEARCH runat="server" id="dnnSEARCH" /><dnn:LANGUAGE
    </tr>
</table>
```

Just like in any tags (HTML or ASP.NET), you have to add attributes to customize how it looks or behaves. For example, on the search, there could be attributes indicating that we do not want to have the radio buttons such as **web** and **site**. Another glaring need would be to add some style to our menu so that it's not transparent and it becomes easier to click on the menu items.

Before we can do any of this, we will need to add an XML file to our skin directory. This XML file will be read in when the skin is parsed. The information stored in the XML file will be matched up with our tokens to add attributes to the ASP.NET tags. As you can see from the preceding figure, the **runat** and **id** attributes are an exception to the rule. Any other attributes would need to be defined.

 XML, short for eXtensible Markup Language is a standards-based format in which data is structured, many times and in this case, in a predefined way. For more information on XML, visit http://www.w3.org/XML/.

Creating Our XML Skin File

Creating our XML file is very similar to how we created our HTM and CSS file in our
`FirstSkin` folder.

1. Right-click on the **FirstSkin** folder and select **Add New Item...**.

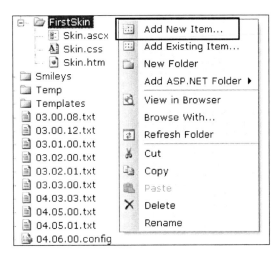

2. The **Add New Item** dialog box should come up. Select **XML File** and type in
   `Skin.xml` in the **Name** field. Then click **Add**.

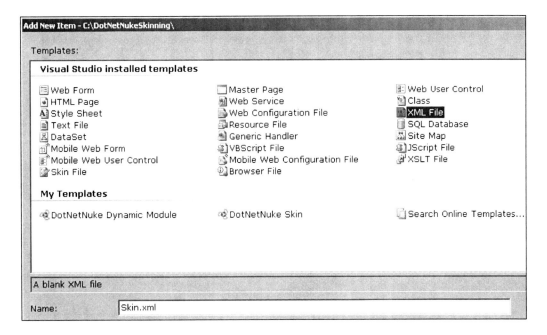

You should now be looking at your new XML file in the VWD code editor. Delete the line of code it puts in there. This is an XML file and will have well-formed XML inside it, but we do not need that XML declaration. DNN expects this XML document to have a root element called `Objects`. This element will have multiple child nodes called object. For example, add the following code to take out the radio buttons from the search box:

```
<Objects>
  <Object>
    <Token>[SEARCH]</Token>
    <Settings>
      <Setting>
        <Name>showWeb</Name>
        <Value>False</Value>
      </Setting>
      <Setting>
        <Name>ShowSite</Name>
        <Value>False</Value>
      </Setting>
    </Settings>
  </Object>
</Objects>
```

The following is an explanation of the preceding XML code:

- There will only be one `Objects` tag as any root node would be.
- Within this one `Objects` tag, we'll have an `Object` tag for each skin object we'd like to configure.
- Within each `Object` element, we'll have one `Token` tag and one `Settings` element.

  ○ The `Token` tag is for those token names we've been using all along. What value we put in there will be used to tell DNN about what skin object to use and is the name we're familiar with.

  ○ The `Setting` tags will represent each attribute and value pair we'd like to add to our skin when it is parsed.

To see the effect of this, make sure you have all the code typed in as it is in the preceding code listing. Save it and go to the skins Admin page to parse it.

Now the **Search** box should not have those radio buttons.

Let's customize the search skin object a little more. Let's say we want to be different from most of the other DotNetNuke sites out there and instead of displaying the text **Search**, let's display **Find This**.

Go back to our XML file and add in a `Setting` element. Inside of it, create a `Name` element with the text `Submit` and a `Value` element with the text `Find This`.

```
<Objects>
  <Object>
    <Token>[SEARCH]</Token>
    <Settings>
      <Setting>
        <Name>showWeb</Name>
        <Value>False</Value>
      </Setting>
      <Setting>
        <Name>ShowSite</Name>
        <Value>False</Value>
      </Setting>
      <Setting>
        <Name>Submit</Name>
        <Value>Find This</Value>
      </Setting>
    </Settings>
  </Object>
</Objects>
```

Parse your skin and view the results.

Do you notice the spacing on the right side of the search skin object? The space is a little scarce compared to the space between the **Search** text box and **Find This**. This looks a little odd.

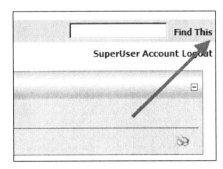

Go into your HTM file and add an HTML space right after the Search token:

```
<td align="right">[SEARCH]   [LANGUAGE] </td>
```

Implementing Style with CssClass

Almost all the skin objects will need some way to implement the style. The attribute called `CssClass` is used for hooking in a style class to both the ASP.NET controls as well as the DNN controls.

Most of the skin objects in DNN are already set up by default to link into the `SkinObject` CSS class. This is great for most of our text- or link-based skin objects, like the current date, breadcrumb, and the others. You generally want these elements of your skin to be uniform.

Let's add the `SkinObject` class into our CSS file to define this uniform style for our skin objects. We'll copy the style that's defined in the `default.css` in the `Portals` folder (`~\Portals\_default\`). Copy the following code from it and paste it at the bottom of our `skin.css` file:

```
SkinObject
{
    font-weight: bold;
    font-size: 8.5pt;
    color: #003366;
    font-family: Tahoma, Arial, Helvetica;
    text-decoration: none;
}
A.SkinObject:link
{
    text-decoration: none;
    color: #003366;
}
A.SkinObject:visited
{
    text-decoration: none;
    color: #003366;
}
A.SkinObject:hover
{
    text-decoration: none;
    color: #003366;
}
A.SkinObject:active
{
    text-decoration: none;
    color: #003366;
}
```

We won't have to add any items to our XML file as our skin objects are already configured to use these CSS classes.

Some of our skin objects are links, and some of them are not. For example, the current date is a skin object and uses the SkinObject class, but it is not a link, whereas the Login skin object is a link. Defining style is a little more involved for link elements as they have different states. That is why we have five different classes defined essentially for what would be one class.

Right now, all skin objects are displayed in the same way regardless of any manner. This may not be what we want, as it may confuse some visitors. We'll keep the links as a dark blue or navy color, and change the other skin objects to a dark gray. The following are the changes in our Skin.css:

```
SkinObject
{
    font-weight: bold;
    font-size: 8.5pt;
    color: #444444;
    font-family: Tahoma, Arial, Helvetica;
    text-decoration: none;
}

A.SkinObject:link
{
    text-decoration: none;
    color: Navy;
}
A.SkinObject:visited
{
    text-decoration: none;
    color: Navy;
}
A.SkinObject:hover
{
    text-decoration: underline;
    color: Navy;
}
A.SkinObject:active
{
    text-decoration: none;
    color: Navy;
}
```

DNN's `default.css` defined its dark blue color with the hexadecimal number #003366. As you can see, we defined ours as `Navy`. Our dark gray color is defined as #444444. For the hover we'll add in underline as the text decoration to affirm to our user that it is actually a link they are about to click on. Save your CSS file and refresh your page.

 You do not need to re-parse while changing the CSS file; you need to do it only when you change the HTM or XML files. If you do not see style changes after adding them to the CSS file, you may need to use the refresh feature of your browser to get it to dump its cached copy and download the new version of the page's CSS file. The refresh that dumps the cache in both IE and Firefox is *Ctrl* plus *F5*.

Skin Objects You Don't See Everyday

There are some skin objects you either haven't seen often or have yet to see:

- [LINKS] — Depending on how you configure it in your XML file, it will either display links to the sibling pages or the child pages. This feature can help search engines and web crawlers to index your site.
- [HOSTNAME] — This skin object displays a link to the host or the main portal of the DNN install.
- [HELP] — This will be a link to the email address of the main administrator of the site you're currently on. This link will not show if the user is not logged in.

When you create a skin, you should decide which skin objects you'd like to include or exclude. These are useful skin objects, so let's include them in our skin. Find the place in our HTM skin file where we have our [copyright], [Terms], and [Privacy] tokens at. Insert a table row right before it, and add these three skin objects separated with pipes (*shift + backslash*).

```
<tr>
  <td style="height:1px;">
    <table class="FooterContainer">
      <tr>
        <td align="center">
          [HOSTNAME] | [LINKS] | [HELP]</td>
      </tr>
      <tr>
        <td align="center">
          [COPYRIGHT] [TERMS] [PRIVACY]</td>
      </tr>
    </table>
  </td>
</tr>
```

Pipes are useful as vertical separators. Let's put some of these in between the [Copyright], [Terms] and [Privacy] too.

```
<td align="center">
   [COPYRIGHT] | [TERMS] | [PRIVACY]
</td>
```

Parse the skin now.

My First Skin Site | Home | About Us | Help
Copyright 2007 by My Website | Terms Of Use | Privacy Statement
DotNetNuke® is copyright 2002-2007 by DotNetNuke Corporation

You may notice a subtle difference in the font used for our pipes inside and outside of the [Links] skin object, because they are not defined by the style that makes them that way. To make them uniform, we'll need to add the class attribute to the containing <td> tags and set it to SkinObject.

```
<table class="FooterContainer">
    <tr>
        <td align="center" class="SkinObject">
            [HOSTNAME] | [LINKS] | [HELP]</td>
    </tr>
    <tr>
        <td align="center" class="SkinObject">
            [COPYRIGHT] | [TERMS] | [PRIVACY]</td>
    </tr>
</table>
```

Reparse and view.

Adding Pages

There are aspects to two or three of our skin objects which are not apparent unless there are more pages in a site. We'll take a look at each of these in a moment, but before we do, let's add some pages to our site. Add a page called **About Us**.

This page will be a root-level page, which means it does not have a parent page. Notice in the following screen shot, the **Page Name** is **About Us**, the **Parent Page** is set to **<None Specified>**, and **All Users** are able to **View Page**.

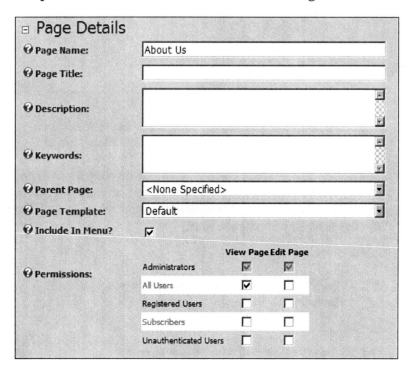

Now we'll add another two pages under this page, one called **Contact Us** and another called **Where We Are Located**. Be sure to set their **Parent Page** to **About Us**.

Navigate to the **About Us** page now. Scroll down to the bottom to see our new skin objects. You can log off to see that the **Help** skin object does disappear when the user is not logged in. This is useful as you don't want to start getting spam by anonymous page scrapings looking for email addresses.

Our **Host** skin object is linking to the DotNetNuke.com site. It does this by default because we have not configured our host site. Go to the **Host Settings** page from the **Host** menu.

The link you put in as the **Host URL** may not work until you deploy it to an IIS server. Right now it is hosted by VWD's internal web server using a random port number which does not make it easy to link to.

If you're on the **About Us** page, you can see by looking at the [LINKS] skin object that it is listing itself and its sibling page, **Home**. Now navigate to the **Contact Us** page and see that its links change.

By looking at the [LINKS] skin object in action, your next question may be how to insert pipes in between the links to stay consistent with the other pipes we used. Thankfully, the [LINKS] skin object is customizable where it comes to this, but we'll need to configure it in our XML file.

In the XML file, add an Object element near the bottom. Set the token to be [LINKS], and also add a Setting/Value/Name pair as shown next:

```
<Objects>
  <Object>
    <Token>[SEARCH]</Token>
    <Settings>
      <Setting>
        <Name>showWeb</Name>
        <Value>False</Value>
      </Setting>
      <Setting>
        <Name>ShowSite</Name>
        <Value>False</Value>
      </Setting>
      <Setting>
        <Name>Submit</Name>
        <Value>Find This</Value>
      </Setting>
    </Settings>
  </Object>
  <Object>
    <Token>[LINKS]</Token>
    <Settings>
      <Setting>
        <Name>Separator</Name>
        <Value><![CDATA[ | ]]></Value>
      </Setting>
    </Settings>
  </Object>
</Objects>
```

For the `Value` of the `Separator` attribute, we've put in the `CDATA` syntax so that the XML parser that DNN uses won't get confused with our space code ` `. We should put in a space before and after our pipe so that it looks consistent with the other pipes. Parse your skin now and go back to **About Us** to see the changes.

The Breadcrumb Skin Object

By default, the `[Breadcrumb]` skin object uses a gif as a `Separator` which doesn't show up very well on our skin, so let's change it. Go into the XML file and add the elements necessary to do this. Instead of using pipes however, let's use an HTML code for right double angle quotes (`&raquo;`).

```
    </Object>
    <Object>
      <Token>[Breadcrumb]</Token>
      <Settings>
        <Setting>
          <Name>Separator</Name>
          <Value><![CDATA[ &raquo; ]]></Value>
        </Setting>
      </Settings>
    </Object>

  </Objects>
```

If you were to parse the skin and view a page, you won't see any `Separator` because by default the `[Breadcrumb]` skin object is not set up to display the location if you are only one page deep from the root and will only display one page if you are two pages deep. Let's change this by adding the `RootLevel` attribute into the XML file.

```
    <Object>
      <Token>[BREADCRUMB]</Token>
      <Settings>
        <Setting>
          <Name>Separator</Name>
          <Value><![CDATA[ &raquo; ]]></Value>
        </Setting>
        <Setting>
          <Name>RootLevel</Name>
          <Value>0</Value>
        </Setting>

      </Settings>
    </Object>
```

The default value for `RootLevel` is `1` which equates to not showing the breadcrumb links until you are one level deep in the site. Setting it to `0` will ensure that it is always displayed. Navigate to the **Contact Us** page now to see our breadcrumb separator.

About Us » **Contact Us**

 You could set the value to be `-1`, and this would display another item called **Root** in the breadcrumb.

Skin Objects' Attributes

What we have done here in this chapter is only a few examples of how you could configure these various skin objects. The following is a listing of all the skin objects that come with DNN along with the different attributes, the default values they are set to, and a brief description.

Token	Attribute	Default Value	Description
[BANNER]	BorderWidth	0	The width of the border around the banner
[BREADCRUMB]	CssClass	SkinObject	CSS Class Name
	Separator	breadcrumb.gif	The separator between the links. This could be text or an image.
	RootLevel	1	The level at which it starts to display the links
[COPYRIGHT]	CssClass	SkinObject	CSS Class Name
[CURRENTDATE]	CssClass	SkinObject	CSS Class Name
	DateFormat	MMMM DD, YYYY	The format of the date
[DOTNETNUKE]	CssClass	Normal	CSS Class Name
[HELP]	CssClass	SkinObject	CSS Class Name
[HOSTNAME]	CssClass	SkinObject	CSS Class Name
[LANGUAGE]	CssClass	NormalTextBox	CSS Class Name
[LINKS]	CssClass	SkinObject	CSS Class Name
	Separator		The separator between the links. This could be text or an image

Token	Attribute	Default Value	Description
	Alignment	Horizontal	Determines if the links are displayed horizontally or vertically
	Level	Same	
[LOGIN]	CssClass	SkinObject	CSS Class Name
	Text	Login	The text of the login link
	LogoffText	Logoff	The text of the logoff link
[LOGO]	BorderWidth	0	The width of the border around the logo
[PRIVACY]	CssClass	SkinObject	CSS Class Name
	Text	Privacy Statement	The text used in the link
[SEARCH]	CssClass	SkinObject	CSS Class Name
	Submit	Submit	What is used to invoke the search? This could be text or an image.
[TERMS]	CssClass	SkinObject	CSS Class Name
	Text	Terms of Use	The text used in the link
[User]	CssClass	SkinObject	CSS Class Name
	Text	Register	The text used in the link. When the user is logged in, this text turns to the user's display name.

If you want to have a more-in-depth look at any of these skin objects, you can go to the ~\Admin\Skins\ path in VWD and find each of them. You can see all the markup and code that constitutes each one.

Summary

In this chapter, you learned about the skin objects and how to customize them in a proper way. If there's one thing that has been lacking in our skin, it is the NAV or menu skin object. Now that we know about the skin XML file and how to add values to it, we're ready to jump in and make it look like a real menu.

6
Configuring the Menu

If there's one thing our skin has needed, it's some style. Now that we understand using an XML file with our skin, we can start adding attributes which will in turn allow us to add this style as well as other settings.

The menu is arguably the most important skin object. It can really add or take away from the appearance of your site. It poses the greatest challenge in making your skin look exactly how the stakeholders imagine it should.

In this chapter, we'll look at the NAV skin object which is the new DNNMenu control.

The New Menu

You may not have realized this, but since the beginning of this book we've been working with the new DotNetNuke menu, commonly referred to as the DNNMenu. From version 2 of DotNetNuke, the menu called SolPartMenu has been the default. The new menu has been designed to be more efficient and flexible.

Here are some quotes from the core team member Jon Henning, the author of both the old SolPartMenu and the new DNNMenu:

> *The SolPartMenu is old and carries a lot of baggage with its almost worth 4 years of backwards compatibility. It has been a goal for v2 of the SolPartMenu to abstract all of the common logic not specific to the menu into separate JS files that could be reused by other controls and applications. This is exactly what the ClientAPI is – an abstraction of logic like positioning, DOM access, XML, etc. The script for the menu should contain only the code for the menu, thus making it easier to maintain and enhance. So in essence, the DNNMenu is in a lot of ways the SolPartMenu v2.0.* (`http://www.dotnetnuke.com/Community/Blogs/tabid/825/ EntryID/16/Default.aspx`)

The following are the new features that have been implemented in the
new DNNMenu:

- **Keyboard Navigation**—You can now use your keyboard arrows to traverse
  the menu items and enter to effectively select an item.

- **Populate On Demand**—This will populate the child menu items when they
  are needed, as opposed to loading them all up when the page loads. This
  reduces the page size and the initial loading wait time.

- **Mouse In Delay**—This slows down the disappearance of sub-menu items
  when you hover off the parent. This can lower the frustration level of users
  using the menu or be quite necessary if there is a spacing gap between your
  parent and the sub-menu items.

- **No Hardcoded Markup**—Hardcoding is typically used as a last resort by
  programmers and was used in SolPartMenu.

- **Option to Remove All Use of Tables**—The menu will use tables for the
  vertical menu items. You have an option of disabling the use of tables.

Initial Menu Configuration

We're now going to start configuring our DNNMenu. Go to your XML file and add
in the necessary elements for the [NAV] token:

```
<Object>
  <Token>[NAV]</Token>
  <Settings>
      <Setting>
        <Name>ProviderName</Name>
        <Value>DNNMenuNavigationProvider</Value>
      </Setting>
  </Settings>
</Object>
```

As you can see, the first setting we'll implement is the `ProviderName`. Let's go
through why this is necessary.

Providers and How They Relate

A provider is a common and shared way of implementing a programming solution.
We're not going to get too deep into the programming theory here, but DotNetNuke
has been designed to use providers for things like communicating to the database,
managing security, and in this case, rendering the menu items. Providers make it
easy to swap out components and functionality.

The `[NAV]` token indicates that the DNNMenu be injected when the skin is parsed, as opposed to the SolPartMenu. However, there is an XML file called `web.config` in the root of ASP.NET sites which specificies which providers to use in DotNetNuke, among other things. For example, if you look at your `web.config` file you will find a line of code similar to the following:

```
<navigationControl
    defaultProvider="SolpartMenuNavigationProvider">
```

In the future, this `defaultProvider` may be set to `DNNMenuNavigationProvider`, but you don't want to rely on what may be set as default in the `web.config`. Besides, you may be selling your skin to a client who may have many portals and many skins installed on his DNN install, and you don't always know what version of DNN they are using. So, be proactive and always set your `ProviderName` for your `[NAV]` token in your XML file.

If you were to parse your skin and view the source of your page output for the menu, you would see something like the following (note that the spacing has been added to improve readability):

```
<span
    id="dnn_dnnNAV_ctldnnNAV"
    name="dnn$dnnNAV$ctldnnNAV"
    HlColor="White"
    ShColor="Gray"
    SelForeColor="White"
    SelColor="Navy"
    FontStyle="font-family: ;
               font-size: ;
               font-weight: normal;
               font-style: normal;
               text-decoration: "
    SysImgPath="/DotNetNukeSkinning/images/"
    Display="horizontal"
    IconWidth="15"
    MODisplay="Outset"
    MenuTransition="None"
    IconImgPath="/DotNetNukeSkinning/images/"
    ArrowImage="breadcrumb.gif"
    RootArrowImage="menu_down.gif"
    RootArrow="-1"
    CSSMenuContainer="main_dnnmenu_container"
    CSSMenuBar="main_dnnmenu_bar"
    SupportsTrans="1">
<xml
```

```
                id="SolpartMenuDI"
                onreadystatechange="
                  if (this.readyState == 'complete')
                  spm_initMyMenu(this,
                  spm_getById('dnn_dnnNAV_ctldnnNAV'))">
          <root>
            <menuitem
                id="36"
                title="Home"
                url="/DotNetNukeSkinning/Home/
                    tabid/36/Default.aspx"
                css="  " />
            <menuitem
                id="57"
                title="About Us"
                url="/DotNetNukeSkinning/AboutUs/
                    tabid/57/Default.aspx" />
              <menuitem
                id="58"
                title=" Contact Us"
                url="/DotNetNukeSkinning/AboutUs/
                    ContactUs/tabid/58/Default.aspx" />
              <menuitem
                id="59"
                title=" Where We Are Located"
                url="/DotNetNukeSkinning/AboutUs/
                    WhereWeAreLocated/tabid/59/
                    Default.aspx" />
            </menuitem>
          </root>
        </xml>
      </span>
```

Noticed the use of XML elements to define the menu nodes? Also, there are no tables being used to structure the menu, at least in the initial page load. Raw data is much smaller than the markup to present the data. It is also good to separate content from presentation any time you have a chance to do so.

Even though you don't see HTML tables here, the DNNMenu dynamically renders vertical menus with tables by default. To see the dynamically generated source in the Internet Explorer, add the following html code to your skin: `<a href="javascript:'<xmp>' + window. document.body.outerHTML+ '</xmp>'">View Generated Source</a>`. This is a simple link, but when clicked on, IE will show you the code.

Basic Menu Attributes

Now that we have set the provider appropriately, let's move on to the common or basic attributes in which you may be interested at first. For our menu, we'll want to keep the default values for most, if not all of these attributes. Even though we won't be changing these values for our skin, it is important you know about these and what they can be changed to if needed.

Attribute Name	Default Value	Description
ControlAlignment	Left	The alignment of the menu within its parent container. Possible Values: • Left • Right • Center • Justify
ControlOrientation	Horizontal	Determines if the menu looks like a typical menu bar (horizontal) or is more like a NAV bar (vertical). Possible Values: • Horizontal • Vertical
Level	Root	Determines the level at which the menu will display the menu items. Possible values are: • Root • Child • Parent • Same
StartTabId	-1	The ID of the page to start displaying the menu items for.
ToolTip	If this attribute is not set, tooltip is not used.	Possible values are: • Name • Title • Description For example, setting tooltip to name will make the page's name display as a tooltip when a user hovers over it.

Setting the Style Attributes

The most commonly configured attributes of the menu will be the ones defining the style classes.

The Sub-Menu Items

The first style attribute we'll set is the CSSContainerSub. This is the attribute which will determine the style of the sub-menu items. Right now if you go to the **About Us**, **Admin**, or the **Host** menu, you'll get the sub-menu items with no background. We'll change this now.

1. Go to the XML file and add the attribute CSSContainerSub.

2. Set the value to be Main_DNNMenu_ContainerSub.

```
<Object>
  <Token>[NAV]</Token>
  <Settings>
    <Setting>
      <Name>ProviderName</Name>
      <Value>DNNMenuNavigationProvider</Value>
    </Setting>
    <Setting>
      <Name>CSSContainerSub</Name>
      <Value>Main_DNNMenu_ContainerSub</Value>
    </Setting>
  <Settings>
</Object>
```

3. Go to the CSS file and add the style class Main_DNNMenu_ContainerSub.

 The reason for giving our CSS class this name is that we could theoretically have multiple DNNMenus in our skin. Adding Main_ would differentiate this main menu as opposed to a secondary menu.

4. Now add the following style definitions:

```
.Main_DNNMenu_ContainerSub
{
    background-color:#dddddd;
    border-right: solid 1px #444444;
    border-bottom: solid 1px #444444;
    border-top: solid 1px white;
    border-left: solid 1px white;
    z-index: 1000;
    cursor: pointer;
    cursor: hand;
    padding: 1px 1px 1px 1px;
}
```

Here is some explanation of the style:

- The `background-color` style will end our transparent menu problem once and for all.
- The four border styles in the preceding code will give the sub-menu items a 3-D effect, where the top and left edges will appear to be catching some light and the opposite edges are casting a small shadow.
- The z-index style will make the menu stand out on top of any elements on the site which may compete for prominence.
- The two separate cursor styles ensure that the hand/link pointer is used for the menu items. We'll use this for other elements of our skin as well as other menu styles.
- The padding style will give a little bit of space around the sub-menu items.

Save the changes to these two files. Parse your skin and verify the changes.

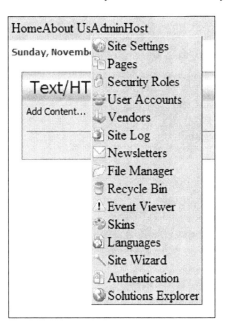

Root-Level Items

The next thing about our menu that may be an eyesore is the fact that the root-level items are scrunched up tightly. Let's now define some styles for these root-level items to make them look right.

1. Add the `CSSNodeRoot` attribute to the XML file.

2. Set its value to `Main_DNNMenu_NodeRoot`.

```
<Object>
  <Token>[NAV]</Token>
  <Settings>
    <Setting>
      <Name>ProviderName</Name>
      <Value>DNNMenuNavigationProvider</Value>
    </Setting>
    <Setting>
      <Name>CSSContainerSub</Name>
      <Value>Main_DNNMenu_ContainerSub</Value>
    </Setting>
    <Setting>
      <Name>CSSNodeRoot</Name>
      <Value>Main_DNNMenu_NodeRoot</Value>
    </Setting>
  <Settings>
</Object>
```

3. Go to the CSS file and add the style class `Main_DNNMenu_NodeRoot`.

4. Now add the following style definitions:

```
.Main_DNNMenu_NodeRoot
{
  cursor: pointer;
  cursor: hand;
  color: #000000;
  font-size: 10pt;
  font-weight: bold;
  font-style: normal;
  font-family: Tahoma, Arial, Helvetica;
  background-color: Transparent;
  white-space: nowrap;
  padding: 0px 10px 0px 5px;
}
```

The `color` style is to set the color of the font. The meanings of some of the other styles are self-explanatory. The one to note here is the `padding`. You could have set the four padding styles as `padding-top`, `padding-right`, `padding-bottom`, and `padding-left`, but we used the shorthand above. When using this shorthand in defining padding, the respective meanings are top, right, bottom, and left. As you can see we set the `padding-right` to `10px` and the `padding-left` to `5px` which gives our root menu items some space.

Menu Items Style

So far we have defined style for sub-menus and the root-level menu items. But we haven't set anything for the menu items themselves. The CSSNode attribute is used for this. Add it to the XML file with the class name of Main_DNNMenu_Node. Moving over to the CSS file, be sure you add it there too with the following defined style:

```
.Main_DNNMenu_Node td
{
    cursor: pointer;
    cursor: hand;
    color: #000000;
    font-size: 10pt;
    font-weight: bold;
    font-style: normal;
    font-family: Tahoma, Arial, Helvetica;
    background-color: Transparent;
    white-space: nowrap;
    padding: 1px 3px 3px 1px;
}
```

Parse, refresh, and view the results. You may not notice a big difference, but you will want this style in there and defined, as you most likely will want to go in and tweak this common style for almost any skin because it defines the non-root menu items. Feel free to change the style for this class and see how it changes the look of the menu items.

Hovering Style

The next thing our menu needs is some change in the background color and/or font when the user hovers over menu items. It adds a subtle level of interactivity so common that it's almost expected in all the menus these days. Add the following in your XML file:

```
<Object>
  <Token>[NAV]</Token>
  <Settings>
    <Setting>
      <Name>ProviderName</Name>
      <Value>DNNMenuNavigationProvider</Value>
    </Setting>
    <Setting>
      <Name>CSSContainerSub</Name>
      <Value>Main_DNNMenu_ContainerSub</Value>
    </Setting>
```

```
<Setting>
  <Name>CSSNodeRoot</Name>
  <Value>Main_DNNMenu_NodeRoot</Value>
</Setting>
<Setting>
  <Name>CSSNodeHover</Name>
  <Value>Main_DNNMenu_NodeHover</Value>
</Setting>
<Settings>
</Object>
```

Then add the following in your CSS file:

```
.Main_DNNMenu_NodeHover
{
    background-color: #bbbbbb;
}


.Main_DNNMenu_NodeHover td
{
    background-color: #bbbbbb;
}
```

Notice that we have two definitions for the Main_DNNMenu_NodeHover class here. The second one is defined for the instances which are <td>'s. Remember, by default, the vertical menus in the DNNMenu are rendered as tables. The vertical ones (the root menu items, in this case) are not rendered in tables, so our first style definition takes care of that one. The hexidecimal value we use here is a slightly darker gray.

Re-parse, refresh, and view the results by hovering over the root menu items as well as the sub-menu items, and see them change as you do so.

Other Styles

You should now feel comfortable with the process of customizing the menu by adding the attributes in the XML file and the corresponding classes in the CSS file. The style we've defined so far will take you to 90 percent of the customization you'd want to set. For the other 10 percent, you may want to reference the following table for a listing of what style can be set and a short description of each. For the sake of completeness, the CSS items we've already covered are contained herein. The DNNMenu attributes are listed in the alphabetic order as follows:

Attribute Name	Description
CSSBreadCrumbRoot	The CSS class that is used for the root-level menu items when they are contained in the breadcrumb listing. If used, it would override the `CSSNode` attribute.
CSSBreadCrumbSub	The CSS class that is used for the sub-level menu items when they are contained in the breadcrumb listing. If used, it would override the CSSNode attribute.
CSSContainerSub	The CSS class that is used for the container of the sub-menu items. This is an attribute we used earlier.
CSSControl	The CSS class that is used for the DNNMenu itself.
CSSIcon	The CSS class that is used for the menu icons.
CSSLeftSeparator	The CSS class used for the left separator of menu items.
CSSLeftSeparatorBreadCrumb	The CSS class used for the left separator when the menu item is found in the breadcrumb list.
CSSLeftSeparatorSelection	The CSS class used for the left separator when the menu item is the page the user is on.
CSSNode	The CSS class used for all the nodes—this is an attribute we used earlier.
CSSNodeHover	The CSS class used for all the nodes when you hover over them—this is an attribute we used earlier.
CSSNodeHoverRoot	The CSS class used for the root nodes when you hover over them.
CSSNodeHoverSub	The CSS class used for the nodes when you hover over them.
CSSNodeRoot	The CSS class used for the root nodes. This is an attribute we used earlier.
CSSNodeSelectedRoot	The CSS class used for the root nodes when they are the selected page. If used, it would override the `CSSNode` and the `CSSBreadCrumbRoot` attribute.
CSSNodeSelectedSub	The CSS class used for the nodes when they are the selected page. If used, it would override the `CSSNode` and the `CSSBreadCrumbRoot` attribute.
CSSRightSeparator	The CSS class used for the right separator of the menu items.
CSSRightSeparatorBreadCrumb	The CSS class used for the right separator of the menu items that are contained in the breadcrumb list.
CSSRightSeparatorSelection	The CSS class used for the right separator of the menu items that is the currently selected page.
CSSSeparator	The CSS class used for the separator of the root-level menu items.

Creating a web menu control is not easy and can take time to develop. The DNNMenu is not an exception. It is the new and upcoming de facto menu to use for DotNetNuke. It does have its shortcomings, which over time will become less and less. Some of the items just dicussed have not effectively been implemented yet. Currently, the items which may not work include the ones involving separators. On August 1, 2006 Jon Henning wrote the following on the DotNetNuke forums regarding the DNNMenu:

> I suspected that the `DNNMenuNavigationProvider`'s code was not complete in its handling of separators, however, the documentation I have says it supports the `SeparatorHTML` properties. Looking at the code shows only a partial implementation in the provider (the `AddSeparator` method does nothing).
>
> I plan on reviewing the DNNMenu and its provider when I have collected enough feedback from the community and can carve out some time.
>
> ```
> http://www.dotnetnuke.com/tabid/795/forumid/109/
> threadid/58074/scope/posts/threadpage/1/Default.aspx
> ```

What he mentions here is to use the `SeparatorHTML` attribute instead of `CSSRightSeparator`. This brings us to the next grouping of attributes to know about which are the custom HTML attributes.

Custom HTML Attributes

The following are some attributes which will allow you to inject HTML markup at key places in the menu, when it is rendered:

Attribute Name	Description
NodeLeftHTMLBreadCrumbRoot	HTML markup added to the left of the node that is in the root and is a page displayed in the breadcrumb.
NodeLeftHTMLBreadCrumbSub	HTML markup added to the right of the node that is in a sub-menu and is a page displayed in the breadcrumb.
NodeLeftHTMLRoot	HTML markup added to the left side of the root menu items.
NodeLeftHTMLSub	HTML markup added to the left side of the sub-menu items.
NodeRightHTMLBreadCrumbRoot	HTML markup added to the right side of root menu items that are displayed in the breadcrumb list.

Attribute Name	Description
NodeRightHTMLBreadCrumbSub	HTML markup added to the right side of sub-menu items that are displayed in the breadcrumb list.
NodeRightHTMLRoot	HTML markup added to the end of the root menu items.
NodeRightHTMLSub	HTML markup added to the right side of the sub-menu items.
SeparatorHTML	HTML markup added between root-level menu items.
SeparatorLeftHTML	HTML markup added to the left of root-level menu items.
SeparatorLeftHTMLActive	HTML markup added to the left of the currently selected, or active, root page menu items.
SeparatorLeftHTMLBreadCrumb	HTML markup added to the left side of the root menu items that are displayed in the breadcrumb list.
SeparatorRightHTML	HTML markup added to the right side of the root menu items.
SeparatorRightHTMLActive	HTML markup added to the right side of the root menu items.
SeparatorRightHTMLBreadCrumb	HTML markup added to the right side of the root menu items that are displayed in the breadcrumb list.

Setting Paths in the DNNMenu

Path attributes are important if, for example, you are trying to get images from a particular path to show up in your skin. The following are the two path attributes you may set:

Attribute Name	Default Value	Description
PathSystemImage	Dynamic path of Control. PathSystemImage	Path of the images for the menu control.
PathSystemScript	Dynamic path of Control. PathSystemScript	Path of the script files for the menu control.

The following are some of the paths you can use that are set within the DotNetNuke system. You may embed these tokens into the values of your attributes in your skin XML file.

Attribute Name	Dynamic Paths
[SKINPATH]	PortalSettings.ActiveTab.SkinPath
[APPIMAGEPATH]	Common.Globals.ApplicationPath & "/images/"
[HOMEDIRECTORY]	PortalSettings.HomeDirectory

Child Image Attributes

The following are some attributes which allow you to set how the menu indicates that there are child menu items:

Attribute Name	Default Value	Description
IndicateChildren	True	True/False value which determines if the menu will indicate that there are child menu items.
IndicateChildImageSub	menu_right.gif	The arrow image to use in the sub-menu items to indicate that there are children items.
IndicateChildImage	menu_down.gif	The arrow image to use in the root menu items to indicate that there are children items.

Future Changes

These navigational controls are changing over time. For example, the DNNMenu may someday be completely free of HTML tables. Or, the horizontal menu items may be implemented with tables. The DotNetNuke code projects (in this case the WebControls project) have been active over a long period of time, and they show little indication that they will slow down in development any time soon. It's a good idea to check up on the status and any upcoming changes to the features or shifts in the direction of the controls we've dealt within this chapter. The following are some recommended links to check or add to your RSS feed listing:

- The DotNetNuke Web Controls Project:
  http://www.dotnetnuke.com/tabid/873/Default.aspx
- Jon Henning's Blog:
  http://www.dotnetnuke.com/tabid/825/BlogID/8/Default.aspx

Summary

In this chapter, we have configured the menu in our skin. We now understand what attributes can be configured with the menu and its related provider. We'll now move on to enhancing our skin design by preparing and adding images to our skin.

7

Images and Web Design

We actually have a skin that we could theoretically implement. But it lacks some pizzazz and eye candy! Without some eye appeal, your stakeholders won't be so happy, and the web viewers may not stick around to check out the content of the site your skin is on.

In this chapter, we will approach the topic of web design with some seriousness. Now that we know the fundamentals of skinning, we need to step it up a notch and create something worth applying to a DotNetNuke site. The meat of this chapter and also the practical details will revolve around images, however.

Choosing a Graphics Editor

Just as Notepad is not the best choice for a code editor, Microsoft Paint is not the choice when it comes to editing graphics for your DotNetNuke skin.

The following are the features needed in the graphics editor you choose:

- **Raster graphics, not vector**: We want to work with the bitmap images, which are considered to be raster-based. Vector-based images, on the other hand, are based on math and geometry to display images.

- **Works with layers**: As you will see that we will be working with several levels or facets of the image. You will need to move and work with these layers independently to get the image you want.

- **Used by most in the industry**: If you have to work with others on a project, you need to be able to work with files they give you or vice-versa. You may be working with a client who will want all the image files, and if you used some uncommon and proprietary format, they may not be happy.

Your Choices

There are many graphic editors to choose from. Some are free and some are not. To see the many choices available you may want to navigate to the following link to see a comparison chart:

`http://en.wikipedia.org/wiki/Comparison_of_raster_graphics_editors`

Here, we will take a look at two of the options:

Adobe Photoshop

Adobe Photoshop is the de facto software used in the graphic art community. This is the editor we will be using in this book. The reason people may not use Photoshop is because of the cost of the licensing or that it is too complex and has a learning curve to use. There is an evaluation version you may download, so the cost shouldn't keep you from at least going through the book examples and exercises. There shouldn't be much of a learning curve in using Photoshop with this book, as we'll be going through each step together.

Here are the links to Photoshop:

- To learn more about Photoshop:
  `http://www.adobe.com/products/photoshop/index.html`
- To download the evaluation or try Photoshop:
  `http://www.adobe.com/go/tryphotoshop`

Gimp

Gimp is commonly used as a free alternative to Photoshop. The great thing about Gimp is that is free and open-source. Another strength is that it can open Photoshop files. Gimp, however, is not widely used as Adobe Photoshop. If you're interested in Gimp but would like it to interface like Photoshop, you should check out the GIMPshop project which aims at this end.

Here are the links:

- **Information on GIMP:** `http://en.wikipedia.org/wiki/GIMP`

- **The official Gimp Site:** `http://www.gimp.org/`

- **GIMPshop:** `http://www.gimpshop.com/`

Begin with the End in Mind

In IT projects, the wise word is to plan and design before you jump in and do the work. This is even more important in creating a great web design. You don't want to start by creating a cool effect and centering your whole site based on that. Take a step back and imagine what the overall picture should look like. Like an artist at a paint easel, you wouldn't blindly stroke the canvas with a green stroke and say, 'that looks like a blade of grass,' and start painting a field.

Creating the right web design can be quite a journey. Make sure you're going in the right direction. If you're a hobbyist, wondering and wasting time may be the luxury you can afford. If you're a professional, time is money, and your competitors will beat you if you're not serious.

Doing Homework

Take a look at other websites out there that will be competing for the web viewer's attention. Compare what you're envisioning with what it will be compared with when it is done. If you are creating this skin for a client, find out what their competitors are doing on their sites in that same industry. If you are creating a generic skin that you will sell across multiple industries, check out the other skins that are for sale. If you're creating a skin for your lovely spouse, get them to tell you what websites they like. Once you find out what your skin will be compared with, design a skin that will stand out above the rest.

Inspiration

Creativity is important in design. If you're not 'naturally creative' or need to be in the right mindset to create and design, you should look at designs or examples that inspire you. Do some web searches for media websites or make a point to always bookmark the sites that make a visual impression on you. When you're ready to be inspired you can always take a look at your bookmarked sites.

If you're going to look specifically at other DotNetNuke skins, I recommend looking at skins the following professionals have prepared. They are among the most respected web designers and skinners in the DotNetNuke industry (listed in the alphabetic order):

- Brian Connor (`http://www.nukeville.com`)
- Evan O'Neil (`http://www.nukeville.com`)
- Nina Meiers (`http://www.xd.com.au`)
- Salar Golestanian (`http://www.salaro.com`)

Also take a look at showcased DotNetNuke sites. You may find a few spectacular designs:

- http://www.dotnetnuke.com/guidedtour
- http://www.dotnetnuke.com/tabid/541/Default.aspx

We're looking for inspiration and some ideas about what is possible. You may decide after reviewing several designs, for example, that you'd like your menu on the right side of the page and that you'll implement dark colors. You should also look at great examples to gauge what quality and level you should be aiming for. You should never copy any design. Doing so without prior consent could get you in trouble.

Purchasing a Design

Don't think you have the creativity to design or start a good skin? You could always purchase or use a free design. Here we will take a look at some of the designs:

Monster Templates

Monster Templates (http://www.MonsterTemplates.com/) is a place to find great designs. There are hundreds of designs. You can browse by category or by your price range.

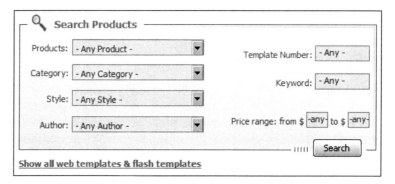

In any case, you should review their licensing agreement before purchasing a design. For example, you couldn't buy a design for $60, make it into a DNN skin, and then sell it to the mass market as if it were your own. You can however use one for a client.

Design Load

Design Load (`http://www.DesignLoad.net/`) has many good templates like Monster Template; however, instead of paying a fee for each template you use, you pay about the same price for usage of their site. For example, you could pay $50-$100 and use hundreds of their templates. The designs may not be quite as good as they are on Monster Templates, but they are still very good. You just can't beat the value. As you can see, there are other design elements you can use besides the web templates:

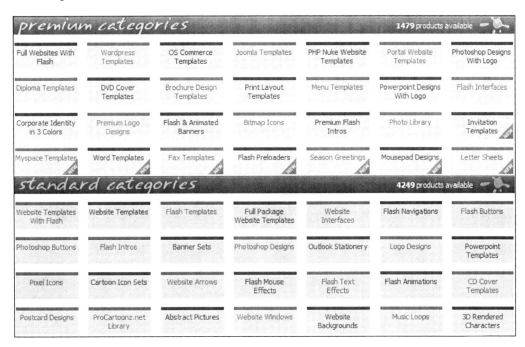

Boxed Art

Boxed Art (`http://www.boxedart.com/`) is similar to Design Load in that is a subscription-based web template library. If Design Load looks attractive, you may want to check Boxed Art out as well and decide which out of both is best for your needs.

Free Designs

Why pay for design templates when you can get them for free, right? Here are some points to consider:

- **Open-Source Web Designs** (`http://www.oswd.org`): This site contains many good templates. One thing better than just being free is open-source. Each template carries their own separate open-source license which is chosen by the designer when it is submitted to the site.

- **Free Web Site Templates** (`http://www.freewebsitetemplates.com`): They would like you to give credit where it is due.

- **Free Web Templates** (`http://www.freewebtemplates.com`): Don't confuse the free templates they have with their image links to their partners. You may want to click on the business link on the left side.

Obviously, there are many paid and free web design template sites out there. If you're looking for more variety, perform a simple web search for web templates and you'll eventually find what you're looking for.

Working with Templates

Generally, you will receive the image files (usually both the web ready and the Photoshop files), an HTML file, and the stylesheets. To create a skin out of it, you'd copy it over to the appropriate DNN directory, then open up the HTML file and put in the skin object tokens. Parse and see where you're at. The biggest challenge here will be swapping out what they are using for the menu with the DotNetNuke menu. There will be of course some tweaking needed unless you want to customize it further.

 While downloading and using a template from any site, be sure to read and agree with the terms of use. For example, some site gives away free templates but requires that you link back to them.

Even if you do decide to use a web template, it's more than likely that you'll find yourself needing to tweak and customize it to your or your clients' requirements. There's also a chance that you only wanted to use a small portion of the design and framed the rest of your skin around it. So, read on!

Design

There are specific points to consider while designing the look of a website (or skin). Think out-of-the- box. Don't start with the idea of this as a DNN site. Close your eyes and start with the idea of coming across a site that really appeals to you visually. Does it have light or dark colors? Does it have a lot of graphics or is it more clean and simple?

Colors

Don't go with 'what looks right' or cool to you unless you have a natural eye for this. You may have an idea of colors in terms of light/dark or a specific color or two, but if you've done web design for long, you'll find that you will need four or five colors to put into a site.

Take a look at a site that will give you a color scheme in which the colors are made to go together (`http://www.colorblender.com/`). In a site such as this, you can specify a color, and get several other colors that complement it.

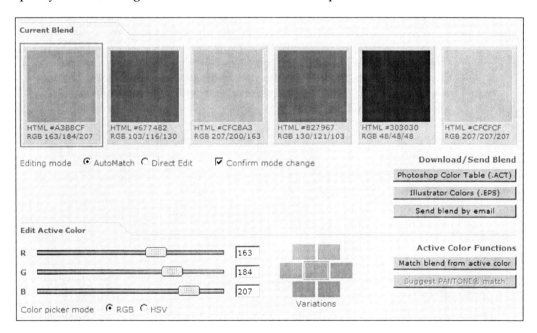

 If you're unsure of the color to start out with, you could head over to their **Browse blends** link (`http://www.colorblender.com/browse.asp`) and look at many color schemes to choose from.

While choosing which colors will be used for what purpose in your design, there are some points to keep in mind: Generally, a light color will draw attention, and darker colors make better for the background color and patterns which add to the scenery, but do not contain any content. While choosing colors for fonts, make sure there is enough contrast between the fonts and what they are on. Nothing will drive a visitor away than the content they have to squint at to read.

While on this page, set the sliders to the values **163**, **184**, and **207** for R, G, and B respectively. This is the color scheme we'll use for our skin in this chapter. Now, click the **Match blend from active color** button. This will give us the rest of the colors we'll use:

- **#A3B8CF**–Light Blue
- **#677482**–Grayish Blue
- **#CFC8A3**—Tan
- **#827967**—Brown
- **#303030**—Dark Gray (almost black)
- **#CFCFCF**—Gray

 Hexadecimal numbers are common for representing exact colors on the World Wide Web. In these numbers, you will notice six characters. The first two define the red element to the color. The middle two define the green element, and the last two, the blue.

We'll use blue colors inside the skin to add some color and for some of the horizontal bars. The tan and brown colors are the bland and darker colors that we'll use for the background. We'll use black and gray for separators and other things that won't draw too much attention to the eyes.

Layout

We learned how to implement the page layout in Chapter 3. We are by no means stuck to a typical layout, however. The sky is the limit and we can create panes if we feel it will add to our overall design.

Banner

The banner (or the graphic used in the logo skin object) is the centerpiece to any design. Be sure it fits in well with the overall design and vice-versa. This is the first thing the user sees when the page loads up.

One important fact to keep in mind is that the banner may not even be included in the skin. The graphic used for the logo or banner is set in the site settings from the admin menu. If you're creating a skin for a specific client or a niche market, you'll want to create most of what will appear at the top of the skin and allow space for the company logo.

If you're creating a generalized skin to be used in many different contexts, you will want to keep the heading part of the skin to be bland so that the owner of the site can have maximum flexibility in inserting whatever type of banner they choose.

Another consideration is whether to allow some additional spacing in the header or banner area of the skin for advertisement banners (the banner skin object). If you don't account for this possibility and the site admin uses them, it could completely mess how the header renders in regard to its spacing. You may in fact decide that your skin will not support any advertisement banners. There are many sites on the net which do not have ad banners or that only use simple text-based ads, like Google AdSense.

Background

Do you like painted or wallpapered walls at home? Do you like solid colors or patterns? One decision to make will be to use a pattern graphic or a solid color. Two other options would be to have a slight gradient of two or three colors or to use one large image which has been popular in MySpace sites.

Bandwidth Considerations

Before we get into dealing with images, you should keep in mind that long loading times gets annoying for viewers. For example, if you like the idea of having one large image as a back drop to the whole skin, be sure to optimize it and make sure it is of a manageable size. Anything over 100-500 kilobytes is considered very large.

Creating Images

It's time to start creating some images for our design. We'll start off with creating a PSD file, then creating our effects and images which we'll then insert into our skin.

Rounded Corners

Although rounded corners are not a big attention grabber, they do add a lot to the appearance of a page or a block of content. Always having straight lines and sporting the common and overused layout that we currently have, shows no imagination or style (no pun intended).

Open up the Photoshop and create a new graphics file.

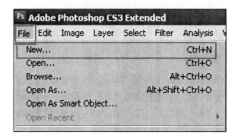

In the **New** dialog box that comes up, enter the following values:

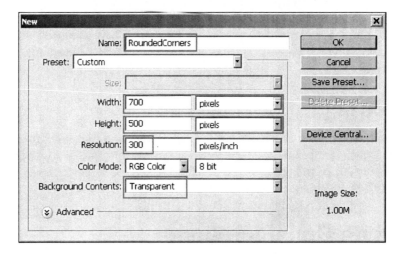

The PSD file we create doesn't have to be the spitting image of our skin design. Most of the skin will still be made up of HTML and CSS. Therefore, we'll create a file that is big enough to work with, but it doesn't have to be as wide as our page.

The first thing we'll do is set the background color on our existing base layer.

1. Go to the **Window** menu and select **Color**. Here we'll double-click on the first color and change what is probably black to our brown color.

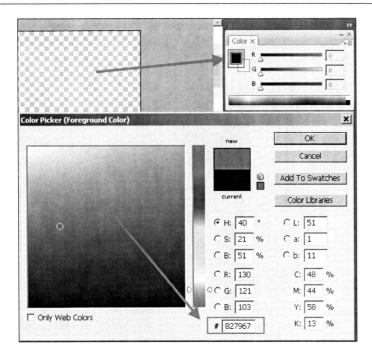

2. Now color in the background with our color by using the **Paint Bucket Tool**. Click on your canvas, and you should see the checked pattern been replaced by our brown color.

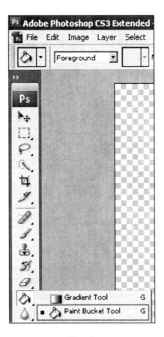

3. Now we'll create the rounded corners. Set the **Foreground Color** to the light brown or tan color. Double-click on the color and bring up a dialog box to choose the color. Set it to **#CFC8A3**.

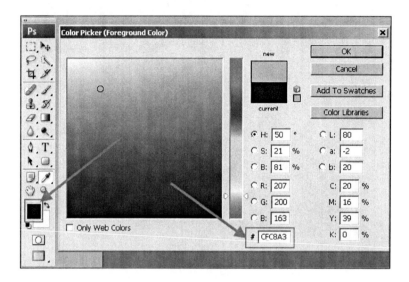

4. Select the **Rounded Rectangle Tool**.

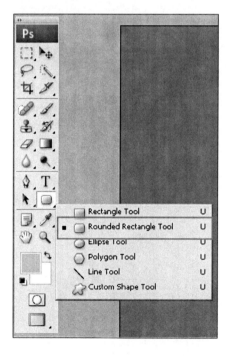

5. Set the **Radius** to be **30 px**. This sets the radius or the size of the corners.

6. Draw a large rounded rectangle. This will create a new layer.

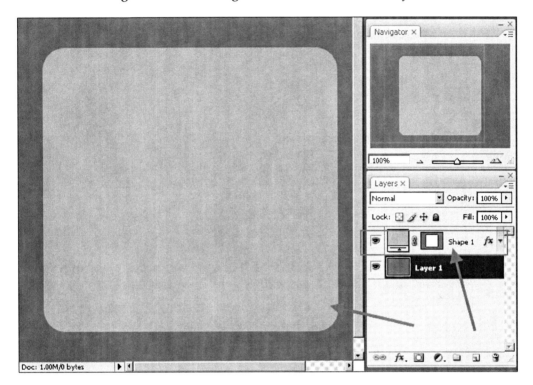

Gradient Bars

Now, we'll cover how to create gradient bars. We'll create several of them, and we can choose which ones and where to use them later on.

A gradient is a transition from one color to another. It can be sharp or gradual. More than one color can make up a gradient. One benefit of using gradients is to add a 3D effect to your design.

Gradients do not have to be in rectangular form. They could be circles, but to keep things practical and relevant, we'll use the Rectangular Marquee Tool.

1. You will probably see the **Navigator** window in the upper-right corner of the Photoshop. If you don't, open it by selecting it from the **Window** menu at the top.

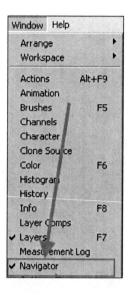

2. Click on the button highlighted in the following screenshot to enlarge your Photoshop image. This will make it easier to draw a rectangle to create our gradient bar.

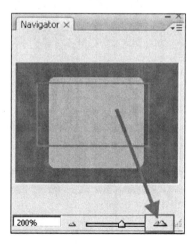

3. Select the **Rectangular Marquee Tool** from the tools window.

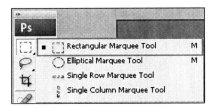

4. Draw a rectangle that starts at one side of our tan-rounded rectangle to the other. You will have to drag your mouse down to the edge, then release. Notice the dotted outline of the rectangle.

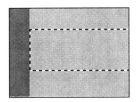

5. Now that we have a selection to work with, we can add a gradient. However, the gradient should be a new and separate Photoshop layer so that we can work with it independently. When the **New Layer** dialog box appears, just click **OK**.

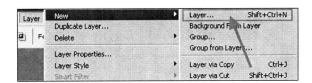

6. Move the newly created layer to the top of the layer stack by dragging it to the top. If we don't move it to the top, whatever we create in it, would be eclipsed by the rounded rectangle layer we created.

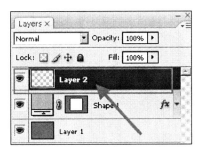

7. Select the **Gradient Tool** from the tools window.

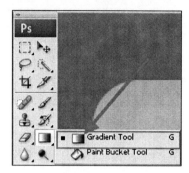

8. Set the two colors in the tools window to be the two blue colors we picked before. Set the darker greyish blue (**#677482**) as the **Foreground Color** and the light blue color (**#A3B8CF**) as the **Bckground Color**.

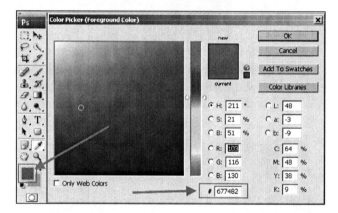

9. With the new layer selected, the rectangle selected (dotted outline), and the gradient tool selected, move your cursor three-fourths down in the rectangle and drag the mouse down. Now use your left hand to hold down the shift key on your keyboard. Drag your mouse to the top of your rectangle, then release.

10. Your gradient bar is finished. Press **Ctrl** plus **D** to deselect your bar.

Now create a second gradient bar by repeating this process, but with the gray colors. This time, however, start in the middle as opposed to three-fourths down. The following are the colors:

- **#303030** — Dark Gray (almost black)
- **#CFCFCF** — Gray

 When creating gradient bars, be sure you make them tall enough to hold what you plan to put in them. In this case, make sure they are tall enough to hold the fonts in our menu.

Shadows and Other Effects

Shadows and other effects that we'll discuss here add more 3D element to your design. Adding these effects are very easy to implement as you will see.

1. Select your rounded rectangle layer.

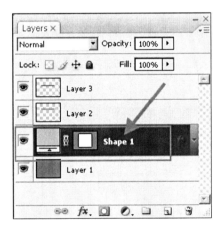

2. Right-click on this layer and select **Blending Options....**

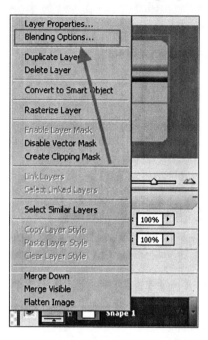

3. Once the dialog box comes up, select the **Drop Shadow** option and be sure it is checked.

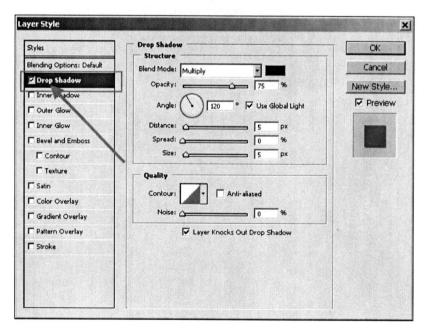

4. Set the **Angle** to **90**. **Distance** to **0**, **Spread** to **10**, and **Size** to **10**.

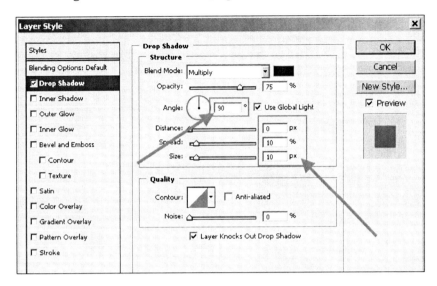

5. Now select **Stroke** from the left side of this dialog box. Be sure it is checked and selected. Set the **Size** to **2**. Double click on the color rectangle and set it to be **#303030**, which is our dark gray color. By doing this, we will give our rounded rectangle a dark, but not too thick outline.

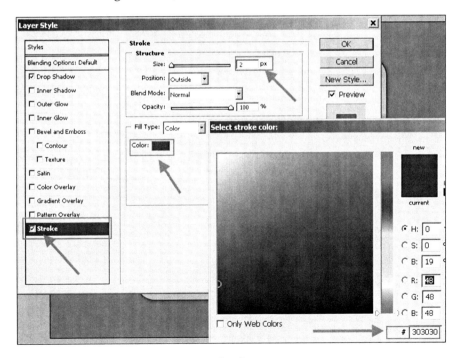

More Photoshop Skills

The various uses of Photoshop and the amazing art you can create with it are vast. Whole books and careers are based on it. How deep and serious you get into Photoshop is up to you. To further enhance your skills in Photoshop, you can go to college for formal training to just follow tutorials you find on the web. Browsing online tutorials is the easiest and is cost effective. Do a common web search or check out a site like **tutorialoutpost** (`http://tutorialoutpost.com/tutorials/photoshop/`) to find some.

Putting the Images into Your Skin

What we have now is a nice web design, but it is in a Photoshop PSD image. We need to break these different elements out into small, usable images for our skin.

Slicing and Dicing

Photoshop has a tool from the tools window called **Slice Tool**. It allows you to break up your one image into several, at defined slice cuts. You then take these separate images and use them in your skin or web layout. Most of our image will not even be used. We need to isolate several points in our image.

Study the next diagram. It shows the parts of the image we'll be using and the parts we will not. Notice that any solid colors will not be used at all. Solid colors can be implemented with CSS and would not require an image download from the browser. Arrows in the diagram denote which slides we'll need. The slices without the arrows pointing to them will not be needed or used (most of which are marked here with X's).

[Slices do not change the image at all. They only specify how the image will be broken up into multiple images when it is saved.]

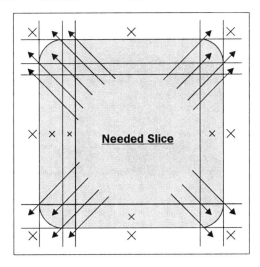

Now that you understand what we need from our image, it is time to learn how to slice to break out these segments into usable images. The following steps will show you how to create slices. You will need to take these steps and apply them further to get every last slice. This is a bit tedious process at first, but after this it will be the old hat!

1. Select the **Slice Tool**.

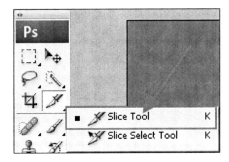

2. Draw a rectangle around your rounded rectangle with the **Slice Tool**. This will start you off with several slices from which to slice up more.

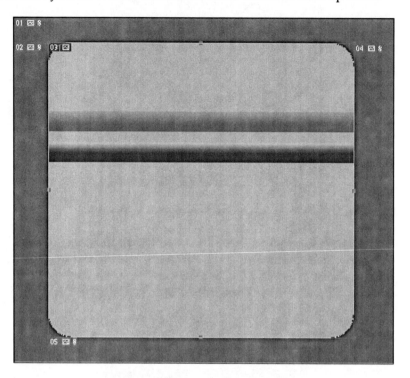

3. Notice that there are dots or squares on the slice lines. You can drag these around to move the slice borders. Move the slice borders to align to the borders of the rounded rectangle.

4. Obviously, we need to break these slices down into more slices. We'll do this by clicking on the individual slices and right-clicking. Do this now on the left side as illustrated next:

5. We'll get a short-cut menu like the following. Select the **Divide Slice...** item.

6. As you can see, once the dialog box comes up, you can divide slices horizontally or vertically. Let's divide this slice horizontally into **5 slices down, evenly spaced**. Uncheck the **Divide Vertically Into** checkbox. Click **OK**.

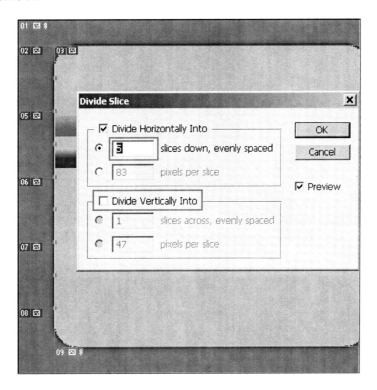

7. Move the edges of these slices to conform to our diagram outlining where they need to be.

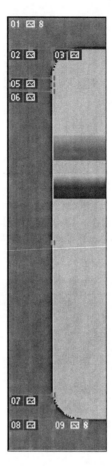

8. Right-click in the very top slice and divide that one into **6** vertical slices. Then position the edges again to match the diagram at the beginning of this section.

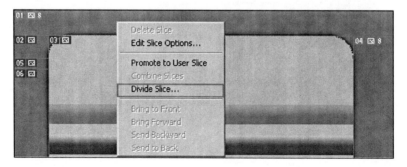

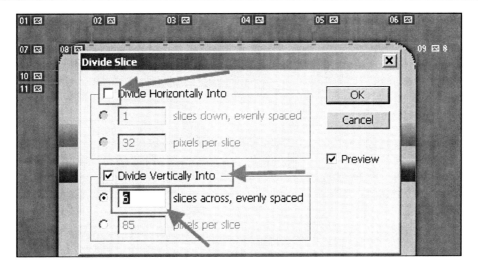

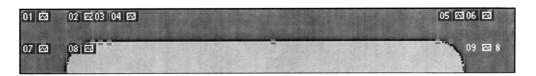

9. Now that you have split and sized both horizontal and vertical slices, you should have no trouble slicing the rest to look like as follows:

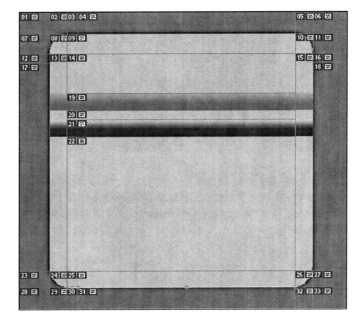

Saving

We are done with slicing and now it is time to save the image. Instead of saving this image regularly which would save it as a PSD file, we need to save it **for web**. However, this doesn't mean that you do not need to save your PSD file. You should save your PSD file as regularly as you would for any other program, like your word processing documents.

Once you are ready to export your image for your web design, you will **Save for Web**. This will not change the original file, its file type, or extension. If you haven't worked with Photoshop, this may seem weird. If you are a programmer, you could think of your PSD file as your source code and **Save for Web** as creating a compiled/usable exe.

1. Go to the **File** menu and choose **Save for Web** (If you have CS3, it will say **Save for Web & Devices...**).

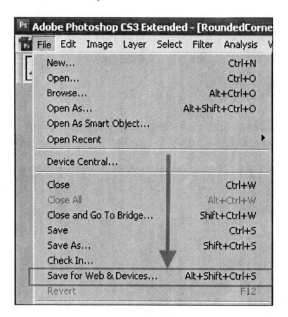

2. Change the **Preset** to **JPEG High** if it is not already set so. You can actually change the **Save As...** settings per each slice, so be sure that each slice has the same **Preset**. After changing the **Preset**, click **Save** and select the **FirstSkin** directory.

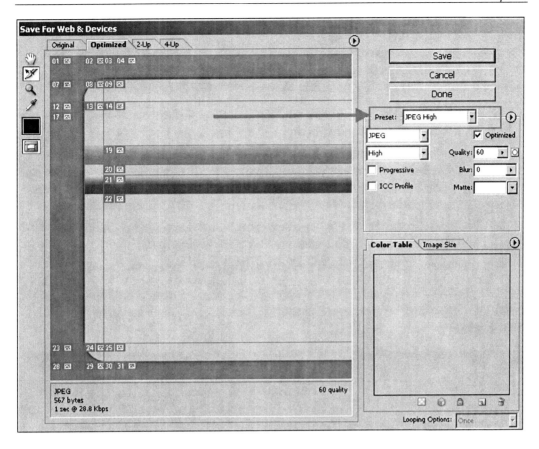

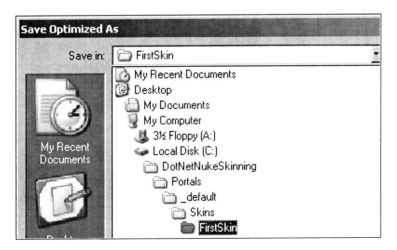

Inserting the images

The challenge in getting our sliced images into our skin is that we'll need to create more table cells for them to fit into. This means a bit of an overhaul on one of the main skin tables. Here are some of the changes we'll need to make to the HTM file:

1. For the sake of space and to make the images seamless, we'll need to add two table attributes (cell padding and cell spacing).

2. Move the control panel into a row of its own. The reason for doing this is because the control panel can take up more width than we want to allow for the space it is at. It could make the middle of our skin more wide and mess up the appearance when we log in. Moving it will take care of this.

3. We'll need to create two rows above and below what we originally have. This will allow for the rounded corners and also the shadows.

4. We'll need to add two more cells on each side of the existing rows.

See the following screenshot. What we currently have is outlined with a thick rectangle. The table borders have been set to show the edges of the table cells involved.

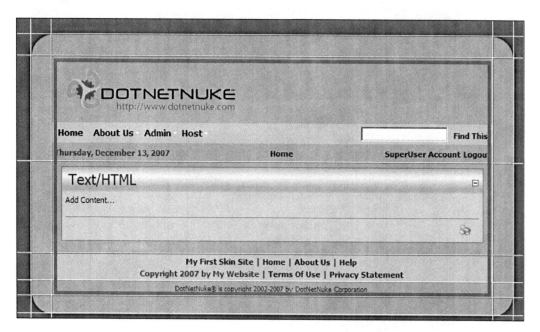

To achieve our first objective, add the following code inside our HTML tables:

```
cellpadding="0" cellspacing="0"
```

Our HTML should now start off like this:

```
<table class="PageContainer" cellpadding="0" cellspacing="0">
  <tr>
    <td align="center">
      <table class="ContentContainer"
             cellpadding="0" cellspacing="0">      .

        <tr>
          <td id="ControlPanel" runat="server"
              style="height:1px;"></td>
        </tr>
```

To move the control panel, we can simply cut and paste it up a few lines, one table up with a row of its own.

```
1 ⊟ <table class="PageContainer" cellpadding="0" cellspacing="0">
2
3
4      <tr>
5          <td align="center">
6              table class="ContentContainer" border="0">
7                  <tr>
8                      <td id="ControlPanel" runat="server" style="height:1px;"></td>
9                  </tr>
10                 <tr>
11                     <td style="height:1px;">
12                         <table style="width: 100%;">
13                             <tr>
14                                 <td>
15                                     [LOGO] </td>
16                                 <td>
17                                     [BANNER] </td>
18                             </tr>
```

The next step is to add in the additional rows and table details needed to display the images we created. If you recall from Chapter 3, our main skin content is made up of five, now four (we just moved one of the rows that contained the control panel) table rows. We'll need to add two new rows before the main content (the four table rows) and two after. Besides this, we'll need to add table details or cells before and after each <td> in each of these rows.

Visually illustrated, the following is what we need:

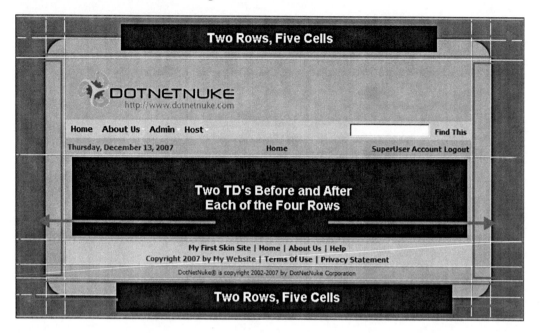

Let's take a look at the highlighted code we'll need to add at the top of our HTM file:

```
<table class="PageContainer" border="1"
      cellpadding="0" cellspacing="0">
  <tr>
    <td id="ControlPanel"
      runat="server" tyle="height:1px;"></td>
  </tr>
  <tr>
    <td align="center">
      <table border="1" cellpadding="0"
            cellspacing="0" class="ContentContainer">
        <tr>
          <td class="SkinSolidBackground"> </td>
          <td class="UpperLeftCornerShadow"> </td>
          <td class="UpperEdgeShadow"> </td>
          <td class="UpperRightCornerShadow"> </td>
          <td class="SkinSolidBackground"> </td>
        </tr>
```

```
<tr>
  <td class="UpperLeftCornerShadow2"> </td>
  <td class="UpperLeftCorner"> </td>
  <td class="TanBackground"> </td>
  <td class="UpperRightCorner"> </td>
  <td class="UpperRightCornerShadow2"> </td>
</tr>
<tr>
```

This takes care of first two rows we need to add. The class names correspond to CSS styles we'll define shortly in our CSS file. These styles will set the image that will be displayed in the cell and will, in some cases, also specify the width and/or the height of the corresponding images. Notice that each cell has an HTML space in it to ensure that it will appear when the page is rendered in a browser.

Now take a look at the highlighted code we'll need to add to the bottom of our HTM file:

```
      </tr>
      <tr>
        <td class="LowerLeftCornerShadow2"> </td>
        <td class="LowerLeftCorner"> </td>
        <td class="TanBackground"> </td>
        <td class="LowerRightCorner"> </td>
        <td class="LowerRightCornerShadow2"> </td>
      </tr>
      <tr>
        <td class="SkinSolidBackground"> </td>
        <td class="LowerLeftCornerShadow"> </td>
        <td class="LowerEdgeShadow"> </td>
        <td class="LowerRightCornerShadow"> </td>
        <td class="SkinSolidBackground"> </td>
      </tr>
    </table>
  </td>
 </tr>
</table>
```

We'll move on to adding the two TD's before and after each of the denoted rows. It is important to understand where in the code these TD's will fit. We just added four rows in total; two at the top and two at the bottom of our HTM file. Look at what is in between these two locations. You should notice those original four rows from Chapter 3 that we added. Each of these original four rows is made up of only one TD or cell. This will change to five, as we're going to add two cells before and two after. These four new cells for each of the four rows will be the same for each row. We'll do the first one together, then you should copy and paste the same code to the other three. The following is the highlighted code to add:

```html
<tr>
    <td class="LeftEdgeShadow"> </td>
    <td class="TanBackground"> </td>
    <td style="height:1px;">
        <table style="width: 100%;">
            <tr>
                <td> [LOGO]</td>
                <td> [BANNER]</td>
            </tr>
        </table>
        <table class="MenuContainer" border="0">
            <tr>
                <td>[NAV]</td>
                <td align="right">
                    [SEARCH] [LANGUAGE]</td>
            </tr>
        </table>
        <table style="width: 100%">
            <tr>
                <td> [CURRENTDATE]</td>
                <td align="center"> [BREADCRUMB]</td>
                <td align="right">[USER] [LOGIN]</td>
            </tr>
        </table>
    </td>
    <td class="TanBackground"> </td>
    <td class="RightEdgeShadow"> </td>
</tr>
```

After you have added the four TD's to the four rows, move over to your CSS file and we'll add the class definitions there. We'll go from left to right, top to bottom.

```
/** 1ST TOP ROW **/


.SkinSolidBackground
{
    background-color: #827967;
}

.UpperLeftCornerShadow
{
    width:27px;
    height:32px;
    background-image:url('images/RoundedCorners_02.jpg');
}

.UpperEdgeShadow
{
    background-image:url('images/RoundedCorners_03.jpg');
}

.UpperRightCornerShadow
{
    width:27px;
    height:32px;
    background-image:url('images/RoundedCorners_05.jpg');
}

/** 2ND TOP ROW **/

.UpperLeftCornerShadow2
{
    width:47px;
    height:30px;
    background-image:url('images/RoundedCorners_07.jpg');
}

.UpperLeftCorner
{
    width:27px;
    height:30px;
    background-image:url('images/RoundedCorners_08.jpg');
```

```
    }

    .TanBackground
    {
        background-color: #CFC8A3;
    }

    .UpperRightCorner
    {
        width:28px;
        height:30px;
        background-image:url('images/RoundedCorners_10.jpg');
    }

    .UpperRightCornerShadow2
    {
        width:53px;
        height:30px;
        background-image:url('images/RoundedCorners_11.jpg');
    }

    /** LEFT AND RIGHT EDGES **/

    .LeftEdgeShadow
    {
        width:47px;
        background-image:url('images/RoundedCorners_12.jpg');
    }

    .RightEdgeShadow
    {
        width:53px;
        background-image:url('images/RoundedCorners_16.jpg');
    }

    /** 1ST BOTTOM ROW **/

    .LowerLeftCornerShadow2
    {
        width:47px;
        height:25px;
        background-image:url('images/RoundedCorners_23.jpg');
    }
```

```
.LowerLeftCorner
{
    width:27px;
    height:25px;
    background-image:url('images/RoundedCorners_24.jpg');
}

.LowerRightCorner
{
    width:28px;
    height:25px;
    background-image:url('images/RoundedCorners_26.jpg');
}

.LowerRightCornerShadow2
{
    width:53px;
    height:25px;
    background-image:url('images/RoundedCorners_27.jpg');
}


/** 2ND BOTTOM  ROW **/


.LowerLeftCornerShadow
{
    width:27px;
    height:33px;
    background-image:url('images/RoundedCorners_29.jpg');
}

.LowerEdgeShadow
{
    background-image:url('images/RoundedCorners_30.jpg');
}

.LowerRightCornerShadow
{
    width:28px;
    height:33px;
    background-image:url('images/RoundedCorners_32.jpg');
}
```

The code in your CSS file doesn't have to be exactly the same, but it should be a close match. For example, depending on how you made your slices, the image file names and the width/heights may be different. You will need to made adjustments based on these differences.

 All your images from your slices should be in a sub-folder called images. If they are not there, move them to make them so.

Adding the Gradient Bars

We have two gradient bars. One that has blue colors and one that has gray colors. Let's now apply the blue gradient bar to the menu.

Because we'll be taking advantage of the image repeating in CSS, our gradient bar image doesn't have to be wide at all. Because of this and the need to keep image sizes as small as possible, you may want to create a new slice to slim it down.

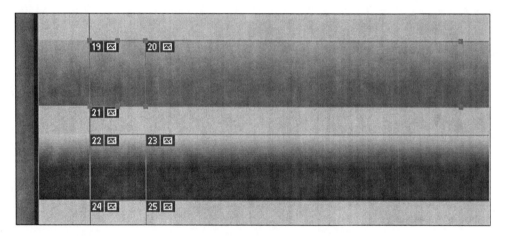

After creating new slices, you will want to re-save the image as JPG's.

We already have a CSS style class set up for the bar that contains the menu. It is called `MenuContainer`. Look at our images folder and find the image which is your blue gradient bar. It may be called something like `RoundedCorners_19.jpg`.

In your CSS file, find the `MenuContainer` class and add the following code:

```
.MenuContainer
{
    background-image:url('Images/RoundedCorners_19.jpg');
    height:33px;
    width: 100%;
    border-top: solid 1px #CFCFCF;
    border-left: solid 1px #CFCFCF;
    border-right: solid 1px #303030;
    border-bottom: solid 1px #303030;
}
```

Notice that we removed the `background-color` from this class. Because we now have a `background-image`, it is unnecessary to keep `background-color`.

If your image name is different, please note that you will need to change the image file name to match what yours turned out to be.

The border entries define a two-shade gray (yes, the gray colors we picked for this design) 3D border around our menu.

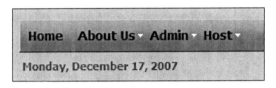

To improve on how our menu looks when you hover over it, add the following highlighted code to your CSS file:

```
.Main_DNNMenu_NodeHover
{
    background-color: #A3B8CF;
}
```

Here we are just changing the `background-color` hexadecimal code (#A3B8CF).

To make our footer portion of our skin to adhere to our color scheme, change the `FooterContainer` class in the CSS file to the following:

```
.FooterContainer
{
    background-color: #CFCFCF;
    width: 100%;
}
```

Here we make the gray color we were using to be the exact light gray color we chose before.

Save all your files and parse your skin. Your skin should look markedly better with the new design.

Replacing the DNN Default Icons and Graphics

If you're willing to affect every DNN portal in a DNN install or the site you're applying a skin to is the only skin in the DNN instance, you may want to change or spice up the images that DotNetNuke uses.

One important point to note here is that this technically does not apply to the topic of skinning, because you're corssing the boundaries of what a skin is. However, being the person responsible for the look and feel of a portal, it might very well fall under what you need to change. The DNN images are used in many places: in errors, in the menus, in core modules, etc. Stakeholders or clients don't care where the line that separates your responsibility as a skinner or a DNN host/administrator is. In fact, they may not even care or know what DotNetNuke is. If it has to do with how their site looks, it may fall on your shoulders.

Summary

In this chapter, we looked at working out a good web design into our skin with images. We implemented rounded corners with shadows and also made our menu look considerably better. Next we'll tackle the default looking containers we've been using up to this point.

8

Creating Containers

You already know most of the concepts and skills needed to create containers. We'll just be applying what you have learned so far for creating containers. In this chapter, we'll be covering the other ten percent of what you need to know to get the job done, and we'll step through the process of creating the containers, one step at a time. Most importantly, we'll be getting rid of the default blue container:

Creating Our First Container

1. In VWD (Visual Web Developer), from the **Solution Explorer** window, find the following location and create a new folder called **FirstSkin**: `~/Portals/_default/Containers/`

2. Add a new item by right-clicking on this new folder. Add a new HTML file and call it `Container.htm`.

3. Similarly, add a CSS and an XML file, `Container.css` and `Container.xml` respectively.

4. Clear out all the code in the newly created files that VWD initializes it with.

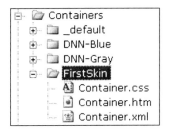

DNN Tokens for Containers

We've worked with tokens from the beginning of this book. These tokens, however, have applied mostly to creating skins, not containers. Containers have their own set of tokens to use here. The following is a listing of them. We'll be working with them throughout the rest of this chapter.

- **Actions**—This is the menu that will appear when you hover over the triangle. It is traditionally placed to the left of the icon and title of the module.

- **Title**—As you can imagine, this is the title of the module displayed in the container. This is usually placed at the top.

- **Icon**—Most of the modules don't have an icon, but many of the administrative pages in DotNetNuke have icons assigned to them. You can always assign icons to your modules, but none of them are set by default.

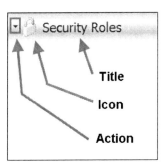

- **Visibility**—This skin object is traditionally displayed as a plus or a minus sign inside a small square. It acts as a toggle to show or hide/collapse or expand the content of the module.

- **Content Pane**—Similar to when we created our skin, this is where the content goes. The difference here is that we have only one content pane. It is required in order to make the container work.

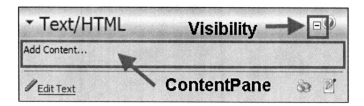

- **LINKACTIONS**—This isn't used very often in containers. It is a listing of links that gives you access to the same things contained in the ACTIONS skin object.

- **PRINTMODULE**—This is the small printer icon you see in the preceding screenshot. When you click on it, it allows you to print the contents of the module.

- **ACTIONBUTTON**—This skin object allows you to display items as links or image links to commonly used items found in the actions menu.

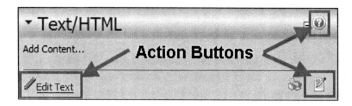

The last item on that list, the **ActionButton**, is different from the others in that we can have several uses of it in different ways. When used as a token, you would place them in your container HTM file as [ACTIONBUTTON:1], [ACTIONBUTTON:2], [ACTIONBUTTON:3], and so on. As you can imagine, we would define what each of these action buttons refer to. We do this in the XML file with an attribute called CommandName. For example, the following is a code snippet of what you could have to add as an action button:

```
<Objects>
  <Object>
    <Token>[ACTIONBUTTON:1]</Token>
    <Settings>
      <Setting>
        <Name>CommandName</Name>
        <Value>AddContent.Action</Value>
      </Setting>
```

```
<Setting>
  <Name>DisplayIcon</Name>
  <Value>True</Value>
</Setting>
<Setting>
  <Name>DisplayLink</Name>
  <Value>True</Value>
</Setting>
</Settings>
</Object>
```

Looking at the `CommandName` attribute, we can have several values which will determine which of the action buttons will be inserted into our container. The following is a listing:

- `AddContent.Action` — This typically allows you to add content, or in this case of the Text/HTML module, edit the content of the module.

- `SyndicateModule.Action` — This is an XML feed button, if it is supported by the module.

- `PrintModule.Action` — This is the printer icon allowing the users to print the content of the module. Yes, this is the second way of adding it as we already have the PRINTMODULE token.

- `ModuleSettings.Action` — This is a button/link which takes you to the settings of the module.

- `ModuleHelp.Action` — This is a help question mark icon/link that we've seen in the preceding screenshots.

Adding to the Container

Now that we know what can be added, let's add them to our new container. We'll start off with the HTM file and then move on to the CSS file.

In our HTM file, add the following code. This will utilize all of the container tokens with the exception of the action buttons, which we'll add soon.

```
<div style="background-color:White;">
    ACTIONS[ACTIONS]
    <hr />
    TITLE[TITLE]
    <hr />
    ICON[ICON]
    <hr />
```

```
        VISIBILITY[VISIBILITY]
        <hr />
        CONTENTPANE[CONTENTPANE]
        <hr />
        LINKACTIONS[LINKACTIONS]
        <hr />
        PRINTMODULE[PRINTMODULE]
    </div>
```

Go to the skin admin page (**Admin | Skins** on the menu). Now that we have a container in the folder called **FirstSkin,** we'll now get a little added benefit: When you select **FirstSkin** as the skin to deal with, the container will be selected as well, so you can work with them as a unit or as a **Skin Package**.

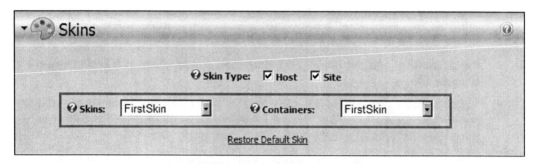

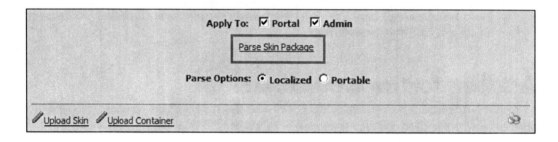

Go ahead, parse the skin package and apply our **FirstSkin** container. Go to the **Home** page.

It may not be pretty, but pretty is not what we were looking for. This container, as it sits, gives us a better illustration of how each token is displayed with a convenient label beside each.

There are a few things to point out here, besides we'll be taking out our handy labels and putting in some structure. Our module has no icon, so we won't see one here. If you go to the administrative pages, you will see the icon. The **LINKACTIONS** is a skin object that you'll use if you don't want to use the action menu ([ACTIONS]).

Table Structure

The structure of our container will be quite similar to how we laid out our skin. Let's start off with a basic table layout. We'll have a table with three rows. The first row will be for the header area which will contain things like the action menu, the title, icon, and so forth. The second row will be for the content. The third row will be for the footer items, like the printer and edit icon/links. Both the header and footer rows will have nested tables inside to have independent positioning within the cells. The markup which defines these three rows has been highlighted:

```
<table border="0"
    cellpadding="0"
    cellspacing="0"
```

```
      class="ContainerMainTable">
  <tr>
    <td style="padding:5px;">
      <table border="0"
          cellpadding="0"
          cellspacing="0"
          class="ContainerHeader">
        <tr>
          <td style="width:5px;">[ACTIONS]</td>
          <td style="width:5px;">[ICON]</td>
          <td align="left">[TITLE]</td>
          <td style="width:5px;padding-right:5px;"
              valign="top">[VISIBILITY]</td>
          <td style="width:5px;">[ACTIONBUTTON:4]</td>
        </tr>
      </table>
    </td>
  </tr>
  <tr>
    <td class="ContainerContent">
        [CONTENTPANE]
    </td>
  </tr>
  <tr>
    <td style="padding:5px;">
      <table border="0"
          cellpadding="0"
          cellspacing="0"
          class="ContainerFooter">
        <tr>
          <td>[ACTIONBUTTON:1]</td>
          <td>[ACTIONBUTTON:2]</td>
          <td></td>
          <td>[ACTIONBUTTON:3]</td>
          <td style="width:10px;">[PRINTMODULE]</td>
        </tr>
      </table>
    </td>
  </tr>
</table>
```

Making Necessary XML Additions

The action buttons we used will not work unless we add items to our XML file. For each of our action buttons, we'll add a token element, then a few setting elements for each. There are three specific settings we'll set up for each: `CommandName`, `DisplayIcon`, and `DisplayLink`. See the following code:

```
<Objects>
  <Object>
    <Token>[ACTIONBUTTON:1]</Token>
    <Settings>
      <Setting>
        <Name>CommandName</Name>
        <Value>AddContent.Action</Value>
      </Setting>
      <Setting>
        <Name>DisplayIcon</Name>
        <Value>True</Value>
      </Setting>
      <Setting>
        <Name>DisplayLink</Name>
        <Value>True</Value>
      </Setting>
    </Settings>
  </Object>
  <Object>
    <Token>[ACTIONBUTTON:2]</Token>
    <Settings>
      <Setting>
        <Name>CommandName</Name>
        <Value>SyndicateModule.Action</Value>
      </Setting>
      <Setting>
        <Name>DisplayIcon</Name>
        <Value>True</Value>
      </Setting>
      <Setting>
        <Name>DisplayLink</Name>
        <Value>False</Value>
      </Setting>
    </Settings>
  </Object>
  <Object>
    <Token>[ACTIONBUTTON:3]</Token>
```

```
<Settings>
  <Setting>
    <Name>CommandName</Name>
    <Value>ModuleSettings.Action</Value>
  </Setting>
  <Setting>
    <Name>DisplayIcon</Name>
    <Value>True</Value>
  </Setting>
  <Setting>
    <Name>DisplayLink</Name>
    <Value>False</Value>
  </Setting>
</Settings>
</Object>
<Object>
  <Token>[ACTIONBUTTON:4]</Token>

  <Settings>
    <Setting>
      <Name>CommandName</Name>
      <Value>ModuleHelp.Action</Value>
    </Setting>
    <Setting>
      <Name>DisplayIcon</Name>
      <Value>True</Value>
    </Setting>
    <Setting>
      <Name>DisplayLink</Name>
      <Value>False</Value>
    </Setting>
  </Settings>
</Object>
</Objects>
```

The CommandName is the attribute that determines which action button is used by the ordinal numeric values. Notice that these four action buttons use different CommandName values as you might expect.

The DisplayIcon attribute is a Boolean (true/false or yes/no) value indicating whether or not the icon is displayed; the DisplayLink is similar and used for setting if the text is used as a link. A good example of both is the **EditText** ([ACTIONBUTTON:1]) in our Text/HTML module on the **Home** page. Notice that it has both the icon and the text as links to add/edit the content of the module.

More Menu Options

Unlike the action buttons, we don't have to have the [ACTIONS] token defined in our XML file, but we'll go ahead and do it for a good reason, which is to set the provider. As we learned in the chapter covering the menu skin object, setting the provider is a good practice, because from version to version and install to install we won't know what menu will be set by default. So we should explicitly declare it ourselves. This is highlighted in the next code snippet.

Add the token definition to your XML file by adding the following code:

```
<Object>
    <Token>[ACTIONS]</Token>
    <Settings>
        <Setting>
            <Name>ProviderName</Name>
            <Value>DNNMenuNavigationProvider</Value>
        </Setting>
        <Setting>
            <Name>ExpandDepth</Name>
            <Value>1</Value>
        </Setting>
        <Setting>
            <Name>PopulateNodesFromClient</Name>
            <Value>True</Value>
        </Setting>
    </Settings>
</Object>
```

The ExpandDepth attribute refers to the menu levels or submenus it will display. The PopulateNodesFromClient is another boolean type of attribute which determines if it will get the menu items when they are needed and populated from the client-side or if they are loaded on the server side, which makes for longer loading times upfront.

Container Token Attributes

Although we won't be adding these in this chapter to our container, for the sake of reference, here they are. The following is a list of some of the skin objects you use in your containers and their corresponding attributes you may add to the XML file with their respective default values and descriptions.

Token	Attribute	Default Value	Description
[TITLE]	CSSClass	Head	The CSS class name used for style
[ICON]	BorderWidth	0	The width of the border around the image/icon
[VISIBILITY]	BorderWidth	0	The width of the border around the visibility icon
	MinIcon	min.gif	The image used for collapsing content
	MaxIcon	max.gif	The image used for expanding content
[PRINTMODULE]	PrintIcon	Print.gif	The image used for printing content from the module

Implementing More Graphics

Now you know how to create containers. There is one part regarding graphics here which has been intentionally left out as we covered it in the last chapter. That is, putting in rounded corners and shadows in our containers. This would keep the look of our containers consistent with the look of the rest of the skin. The steps needed to accomplish this are almost exactly the same from the last chapter:

1. Create a PSD file in PhotoShop.
   - Create a rounded rectangle with the appropriate colors. This time the background color will match with the tan color.
   - Create the shadow effect.
2. Save the sliced images in Photoshop.
3. Create two rings of table cells around what you have already got, and set their widths and heights to match the respective images.
4. Insert the images using CSS.

Summary

You now know how to create containers. Your DotNetNuke skinning skills are almost complete. Next, we'll cover how to package our skins.

9 Package and Deploy

You have now been exposed to and know all the parts to creating skins, except for packaging and preparing it for prime time use. Once you're ready to use your skin on a production DotNetNuke site, you will want to package and then upload it. In this chapter, we will learn how to create a thumbnail for our skin and containers. We will go over how to pack up our skin into a zip file and how to install a skin with this zip file. Finally, we will cover how to handle any errors after applying a skin.

What is Packaging?

Packaging, in regard to skinning, is the act of putting all of the files that make up the skin (HTM, CSS, XML, graphic files, etc.) into one zip file. This makes it easy to move the skin around as a whole and to upload/install it into a DotNetNuke install. There are essentially two types of packages, one for the skin itself and one for the container. They can be packaged and uploaded together or separately.

Is Packaging Necessary?

Packaging your skin is not necessary to use the skin, as you have seen throughout this book. Packaging is also not necessary to move or deploy your skin on another DotNetNuke install or a different server. For example, once you have created the folders (as we have in this book) and a copy of the files that make up your skin, it is deployed and can be applied to a DNN portal. If this is true, why then would you want to package your skin?

You will want to package your skin to make it easy for others to use your skin in their DotNetNuke portal. It is also easier for you to upload your skin package to a DNN install rather than using an FTP client to move the files.

How to Package

Packaging skins is so easy, it can be explained in one statement: Zip your files into a file!

Now we'll step through this simple process:

1. Open up **Windows Explorer** by double-clicking on **My Computer** on your desktop. You can also find it on the **Start** menu, under **Accessories**.
2. Go to your skin in your local DNN install location which should be found at `C:\DotNetNukeSkinning\Portals\_default\Skins\FirstSkin`.
3. Select all your skin files along with your images folder. Exclude the ASCX file as this will be generated and will not be needed later on.
4. Right-click on the following selection of items and hover over **Send To**, then select **Compressed (zipped) Folder**.

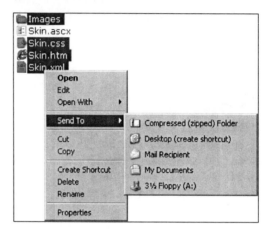

5. That should have created a zip file with the name `Skin.zip`. Rename it to be `DeployedFirstSkin.zip`.
6. Now let's zip up the container files into a separate zip file. Go to `C:\DotNetNukeSkinning\Portals\_default\Containers\FirstSkin`.
7. Select all your container files along with any images folder. Exclude the ASCX file as this will be generated and will not be needed later on. This should have created a file called `container.zip`. Rename it to be `DeployedFirstSkin.zip`.

The two files we just created were your skin and container package files respectively. The name you give the zip file is the name DotNetNuke will give it when you upload it to a DNN install. As we already have a skin called `FirstSkin` and we'll use this same DNN instance to test it on, we renamed it with a different name.

How to Deploy

Let's step through the process you need to deploy this skin package:

1. Click on the **Host** menu and go to the **Skins** page.

2. From there, click on the **Upload Skin** link. This will take you to a page where you will specify the skin zip file.

3. Click **browse** and select the zip file in the skin directory: C:\ DotNetNukeSkinning\Portals_default\Skins\FirstSkin.

4. Then click **Install Skin Package**.

5. Click the back button once this is done, or simply navigate back to the **Skins** Host page.

6. Now we'll deploy our containers package by clicking on **Upload Container**.

7. Select our zip file from the **C:\DotNetNukeSkinning\Portals_default\ Containers\FirstSkin** directory.

8. Click the **Upload Container Package**.

9. Again go back to the Host **Skins** page and verify that both the skin and the container appear in the appropriate drop-downs.

 If you like the idea of creating one package file for both the skin and the container, you can name your skin package as Skin.zip and your container package as Container.zip. Zip these two files into one file called DeployedFirstSkin.zip. When you upload this one file, DNN will see that it contains both and will parse it appropriately.

Creating Thumbnails

What you may have noticed as lacking when you look at our skin and container in the **Skins** administrative page is that we have no thumbnail images to represent them. We need to create simple screenshots of our skin and container and include them into our packages.

Let's do this now:

1. Go to your Home page in the Internet Explorer and press *Alt* plus *Prt Scr*. This will copy the image of the page onto the Windows clip board.

2. Open up a graphics editor like MS Paint. You can use Photoshop if you like to.

3. Crop the image a little to make the appearance better and to just get how the skin looks without the sides of the browser.

4. Save this image as `Skin.jpg` into our `FirstSkin` Directory we've been working in. It should be named with the same name of the skin and should also be a JPG.

5. In the Windows Explorer, drag this JPG file onto the ZIP file. This should automatically add this graphic to the ZIP package.

6. Follow the steps from the previous section to redeploy the package.

This time around, the thumbnail should show up fine. Repeat the above steps for the container package. You may want to crop further to just include the appearance of the container, rather than the whole skin.

Handling Bad Installs

There are times when things don't go right. Typically, this happens much more with new module installs than skin packages, but you should be ready to handle the problem if one arises.

Let's say we started using this new skin called `DeployedFirstSkin`, and we made some changes to it and needed to upload the package again. This time, the changes we made were not desirable and possibly caused an error when DNN processed your ASCX file while rendering your skin. Because your skin was already applied to the current portal, you may not be able to get to the administrative **Skin** page to change the skin to make DNN operable again.

Do not fear! Knowing what we do about ASCX files, we can simply go into a skin we know is fine and "copy and paste" the code from its ASCX file into ours or FTP it over ours. This will make DotNetNuke operable again, so you can go in and fix the problem with your skin.

Summary

The logistics of deploying our skins may have been a big deal in your mind before reading this chapter, but now you probably realize how fast and easy it is to do. You now know how to package and also how to handle any runtime errors that may come up.

10
Skinning the Control Panel

Traditionally, the control panel is not a part of the DotNetNuke skin. It is only seen by administrators or super users after they have logged in. However, there are reasons why you might need to change the appearance of the control panel. For example, you may be a contracting consultant setting up a DNN install for business owners and want to match the control panel with the rest of your skin theme. Perhaps you'd like to eliminate buttons or links that aren't used by your site administrators, and would like to streamline things a bit. We will take a look at how to do it in this chapter.

Your Choice of Control Panels

You may or may not know that you have a choice in the control panels you use for your DotNetNuke install. Go to your **Host** menu to go to **Host Settings**. Expand **Advanced Settings**, then **Other Settings**. There is an item there called **Control Panel**. Notice you have two choices. Set the value to be **CLASSIC**, and then save the settings. The default is **ICONBAR**. Notice how the classic control panel is different. It is smaller and simpler.

The **ICONBAR** control panel is the choice of the majority, so we'll set it back and modify that one. Set it back to **ICONBAR** now.

Control Panel—In Detail

The control panel is not a part of the DotNetNuke skin. Thus, we will not be setting CSS styles in a CSS file that is a part of the skin. To do so would not be smart considering those changes would go away when the skin is changed. We can, however, change the `default.css` in the `~\Portals\_default` location. We'll be doing this in a moment. We can also change the files that make up the control panel.

The location of the control panels is at `~\admin\ControlPanel`. Open up Windows Explorer and go to this location and notice files named after IconBar and Classic.

Name	Size	Type ▲	Date Modified
App_LocalResources		File Folder	9/26/2007 5:27 PM
images		File Folder	9/26/2007 5:27 PM
classic.ascx	4 KB	ASP.NET User Control	9/12/2007 12:00 AM
iconbar.ascx	12 KB	ASP.NET User Control	9/12/2007 12:00 AM
Classic.ascx.vb	13 KB	VB File	9/12/2007 12:00 AM
IconBar.ascx.vb	24 KB	VB File	9/12/2007 12:00 AM

A word of caution: Changing these files is considered to be *changing the core* of DotNetNuke. At this point, we are not *making a skin* or *developing a module* for DotNetNuke. We are *changing* DotNetNuke. There are two ways to take this. First, become dogmatic and insist that the core of your DNN install remains unchanged. Second, understand some fundamentals, relax, and change it anyway.

There is no shame in insisting to not change the core. If you want to play it safe and decide changing the control panel is not that important, you may want to stop at this point and not move on with this chapter.

We'll go over some fundamentals if you choose to proceed. The first is to understand the value of backups. If you're a technically savvy computer user, you already know the importance of backups and implement them in ensuring that valuable data is kept safe in case of a hard disk failure or some other disaster. Here, we want to ensure we can always go back to the way things were, in case we 'mess things up.' Regardless, it is always a good idea to perform a backup of your DotNetNuke install before making a change to your DotNetNuke install. This is no exception.

To backup your DotNetNuke install files, open Windows Explorer and right click on the root folder of the install. Choose **Send To | Compressed (zipped) Folder**. This may take a few moments, but will create a zip file which will contain all your files for that moment in time. You now have a backup.

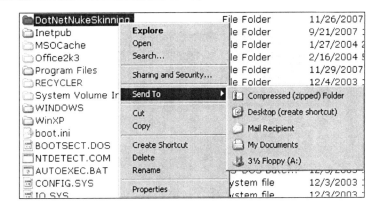

To have a more complete backup of your DotNetNuke install, you should make a backup of your SQL Server database as well. If you have set up DNN as outlined in this book, you have just done this as the database files were created in the folder App_Data. If you did not set up your DNN according to the steps outlined in this book, you need to find where the mdf file is located and back it up too.

Another fundamental to realize is that the ASCX files contain markup, both HTML and ASP.NET. The VB files are Visual Basic code files which are compiled and reference items that were defined in the ASCX file. As we move on, we'll make note of these and the consequences of changing them.

The last concept to understand is if you plan to upgrade your version of DotNetNuke in the future, you will need to make sure your changes are compatible with the new versions. Provided that the core team does not make significant changes to how the control panel or the items therein are referenced, you should have no trouble. In a worst case scenario, you'll just be going back to the default control panel when upgrading.

Change the Background Color

The first change we'll make to our control panel is the background color. As the control panel already references style classes defined in the default.css, we can easily and quickly make effective changes there.

Using VWD, go to the ~\Portals_default folder and open the default.css file. You should see an entry for the control panel. Change its background-color value to #CFC8A3. Save the code file. Go to Internet Explorer and refresh the page. You should see a change in your control panel's background color.

Let's change the border of the control panel too. Going back into `default.css`, you should see four border entries in the `ControlPanel` class. Change the hexadecimal numbers to this #303030. Also change the border width of the border to 2 px. See the following:

```
.ControlPanel, .PagingTable
{
    width: 100%;
    background-color: #CFC8A3;
    border-right:   #303030 2px solid;
    border-top:     #303030 2px solid;
    border-left:    #303030 2px solid;
    border-bottom:  #303030 2px solid;
}
```

Save and view the modified control panel in the browser.

Streamline the Control Panel

You may come to have your own reasons to streamline the control panel. One known issue people have with it is that some of the drop-down lists are too narrow. Another issue is that the common tasks section is redundant because you can get to these items from the Admin or Host menu. We'll modify these two aspects now.

Lengthen the Module Drop-Downs

If you install many third-party modules, or start to rename modules to organize them more, you'll soon learn the space in the module drop-down list is too narrow.

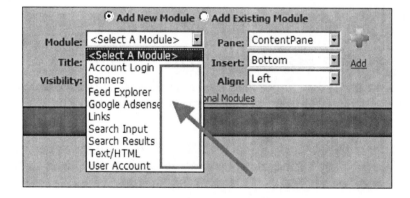

Using VWD, go to the `~\admin\ControlPanel` folder and open up the `iconbar.ascx` file. Press *Ctrl* plus *F* to bring up the find dialog box. Type in `cboDesktopModules` as the text to search for, and then press *Enter*. This will find us the ASP.NET drop-down control to widen that holds the module names.

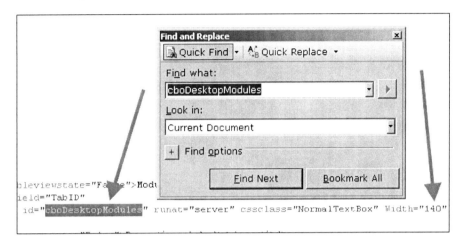

You can see the current `Width` of this drop-down list is `140` pixels. Change this number to be `220`. Save the code file, and then view the changes in the browser window.

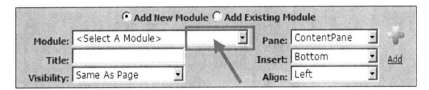

Although we have a nice wide **Module** drop-down list, it doesn't look quite right with the **Title** and **Visibility** controls below it with less width. We should make those just as wide to make it visually appealing.

Do you see the two radio buttons at the top of the previous screenshot—**Add New Module** and **Add Existing Module**? Based on which of these two buttons is selected, the controls underneath will change, except for the **Visibility**. So, instead of having to modify only three controls, we'll have to modify five.

Here is how we can make the visual adjustment:

- Do a search for `cboTabs`, which is the other **Module** drop-down. Change its `Width` to 220.

- Perform another search for `cboModules`, which is the title for the **Title** when it is a drop-down list. Set its `Width` to 220.

- Next, search for `txtTitle`, which is the title for the **Title** when it is a text box. Set its `Width` to 220.

- Now do a search for `cboPermission`, which is for the **Visibility** drop-down. Set its `Width` to 220.

- Save your changes and view the effect in the browser.

Eliminate Common Tasks

There are many DNN users who never use the links underneath **Common Tasks**. If you and your users are among those who don't., you may want to eliminate the section altogether from the control panel.

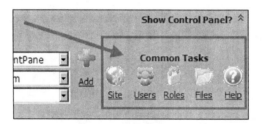

Perform a search (*Ctrl* plus *F*) for the control named `lblCommonTasks`. Locate the line above that one, which is a `td` tag. We want to hide this `td` as it contains the section we want to delete. We want to hide it instead of deleting it because there is code in the underlying `.vb` file that references the items contained in it. Deleting the markup code references would result in fatal run-time errors, so we'll hide it instead.

Go to the `style` attribute and add `display:none;` as the style definition.

```
utton id="cmdInstallModules" runat="server" cssclass="CommandButton" CausesVa
ter" valign="middle" style="border-top:1px #CCCCCC dotted;display:none;">
ID="lblCommonTasks" Runat="server" CssClass="SubHead" enableviewstate="false
lspacing="0" cellpadding="2" border="0">
lign="bottom" height="24">
```

If you were to save and view the result in a browser, you would see that the Common Tasks are truly gone but the module controls in the middle are still sitting in the same spot and not taking up some of the new space we just created.

Now, perform a search on `optModuleType` so that we can find the `td` that contains the module drop-down controls. We'll set the `colspan` of that `td` to be `2`, so it will take up the space the other cell occupied.

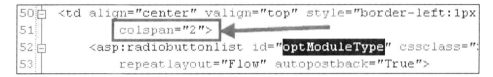

Save and view your new control panel.

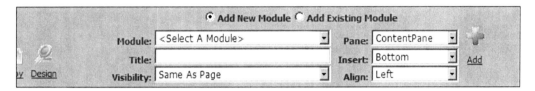

Summary

In this chapter, we looked at how to modify a core component of DotNetNuke — the control panel. We learned how to make some cosmetic changes through `default.css` and how to modify the ASCX file that makes up the control panel. You should now understand how to make other such cosmetic changes to match the control panel with a particular skin by looking at the examples we used.

You have reached the end of the book. I hope you have enjoyed the journey and have created just your first of many great DotNetNuke skins.

Index

O

open-source web designs, free designs 84

P

packaging
  about 129
  importance 129

R

root-level items, style attributes 71, 72

S

skin
  about 5
  code, modifying 32-34
  components 7
  creating 11
  editing 28
  file types 8
  gradient bars, adding 114, 115
  images, adding into 98
  images, inserting 106-114
  images, slicing 98
  objects 6, 7
  packaging 129, 130
  parsing 23
  parsing, need for 23
  skin objects, adding 58
  steps, for creating 9
  structure 6
  style, implementiing through CSS 42-44
  table structure, designing 30, 31
  thumbnails, crreating 131
  VWDs designer tools 30, 31
  XML file, creating 53-55
skin, creating
  development environment, setting up
      15-18
  DotNetNuke install, creating 15, 16
  DotNetNuke starter kits, installing 13
  editor, selecting 11
  VWD (Visual Web Developer), installing
      11, 12, 13

skinning
  about 5
  features 9
skin objects
  [HELP] 58
  [HOSTNAME] 58
  [LINKS] 58
  about 49
  attributes 63, 64
  breadcrumb skin object 62, 63
  customizing 51, 52
  style, implementing with CSS class 56-58
SolPartMenu 65
style attributes, DNNMenu
  custom HTML attributes 76, 77
  hovering style 73, 74
  menu items style 73
  other style 74
  root-level items 71
  sub-menu items 70, 71

T

table structure, containers 123, 124

V

VWD (Visual Web Developer), installing
      11-13

X

XML, file types 9

Packt Open Source Project Royalties

When we sell a book written on an Open Source project, we pay a royalty directly to that project. Therefore by purchasing DotNetNuke Skinning Tutorial, Packt will have given some of the money received to the DotNetNuke project.

In the long term, we see ourselves and you—customers and readers of our books—as part of the Open Source ecosystem, providing sustainable revenue for the projects we publish on. Our aim at Packt is to establish publishing royalties as an essential part of the service and support a business model that sustains Open Source.

If you're working with an Open Source project that you would like us to publish on, and subsequently pay royalties to, please get in touch with us.

Writing for Packt

We welcome all inquiries from people who are interested in authoring. Book proposals should be sent to authors@packtpub.com. If your book idea is still at an early stage and you would like to discuss it first before writing a formal book proposal, contact us; one of our commissioning editors will get in touch with you.

We're not just looking for published authors; if you have strong technical skills but no writing experience, our experienced editors can help you develop a writing career, or simply get some additional reward for your expertise.

About Packt Publishing

Packt, pronounced 'packed', published its first book "Mastering phpMyAdmin for Effective MySQL Management" in April 2004 and subsequently continued to specialize in publishing highly focused books on specific technologies and solutions.

Our books and publications share the experiences of your fellow IT professionals in adapting and customizing today's systems, applications, and frameworks. Our solution-based books give you the knowledge and power to customize the software and technologies you're using to get the job done. Packt books are more specific and less general than the IT books you have seen in the past. Our unique business model allows us to bring you more focused information, giving you more of what you need to know, and less of what you don't.

Packt is a modern, yet unique publishing company, which focuses on producing quality, cutting-edge books for communities of developers, administrators, and newbies alike. For more information, please visit our website: www.PacktPub.com.

Building Websites with VB.NET and DotNetNuke 4

ISBN: 1-904811-99-X   Paperback: 350 pages

A practical guide to creating and maintaining your own DotNetNuke website, and developing new modules and skins

1. Specially revised and updated version of this acclaimed DotNetNuke book

2. Create and manage your own website with DotNetNuke

3. Customize and enhance your site with skins and custom modules

4. Extensive coverage of the DAL and DAL+ for custom module development

---

Drupal 5 Themes

ISBN: 978-1-847191-82-3   Paperback: 250 pages

Create a new theme for your Drupal website with a clean layout and powerful CSS styling

1. Learn to create new Drupal 5 Themes

2. No experience of Drupal 5 theming required

3. Set up and configure themes

4. Understand Drupal 5's themeable functions

Please visit **www.PacktPub.com** for information on our titles

Printed in the United States
123826LV00003B/85/P

9 781847 19278